# THE COWARD?

**By the same author:**

*The Scapegoat; the life and tragedy of a Fighting Admiral and Churchill's role in his death*, Book Guild Publishing, 2014

www.steverdunn.com

# THE COWARD?

*The Rise and Fall of The Silver King*

Steve R. Dunn

Book Guild Publishing
Sussex, England

First published in Great Britain in 2014 by
The Book Guild Ltd
The Werks
45 Church Road
Hove, BN3 2BE

Typesetting in Garamond by
YHT Ltd, London

Printed and bound in Great Britain by
CPI Group (UK) Ltd, Croydon, CR0 4YY

A catalogue record for this book is available from
The British Library.

ISBN 978 1 909984 62 2

*This book is dedicated to Vivienne, who believed.*

Man gives every reason for his conduct save one, every excuse for his crimes save one, every plea for his safety save one; and that one is his cowardice.

George Bernard Shaw (1856–1950), *Man and Superman*, 1903

# The Troubridge Arms and Motto

*Ne cede arduis* – 'Yield to no difficulty'.

Arms: *Out of waves, a bridge of three arches embattled, surmounted by a tower proper, thereon a broad pennon flying azure, charged with a cross polent of the field, on a canton of the third, two keys in saltire, wards upward gold.*
Mantling: *Azure and or.*
Crest: *On a wreath of the colours a dexter arm embowed, habited azure, cuffed argent holding a banner azure charged as the canton.*

# *Contents*

# Preface

What is cowardice? Is it the opposite of bravery? Does it have a moral as well as a physical dimension? Can a brave man also be a coward? Are we all cowards under the skin, a desperate need for self-preservation being the key motivating factor in most human behaviour and fear its manifestation? Survival, after all, depends on us being able to recognise and categorise risk so that we can avoid it and hence live to propagate our genes.

The seventeenth-century English philosopher Thomas Hobbes thought fear to be part of the natural condition. In *Leviathan* he wrote that when his mother bore him she gave birth to twins, Hobbes himself and fear. He delighted in his timidity and was a fearful man all his life. John Locke, the important Enlightenment thinker, thought that an officer had the right to kill a soldier who was a coward, for otherwise all would avoid hardship. The Prussian philosopher of Absolute Idealism, Georg Hegel, posited that the state had the right to demand that its citizens lay down their lives for its survival. To refuse was cowardice.

The horrendous death toll of the First World War was prefigured by the American Civil War of 1861–1865, in which some 750,000 soldiers died together with a large number of civilians. It was estimated that the death toll accounted for 10% of all Northern males aged 20–45 and 30% of all Southern white males aged 18–40. Beginning as a war in which determined infantry could successfully charge and overrun entrenched positions at the point of a bayonet, by its close the advance of technologies such as effective field artillery and breech loading rifles made such charges murderous.

Soldiers threw away their weapons more willingly than the entrenching tools which could create for them some feeble shelter and high rates of desertion crippled the Confederate forces in their final days.

By the advent of the First World War in 1914 such technological advances, ignored by the generals and politicians commanding the opposing armies, placed flesh and blood at the mercy of high explosive and machine guns. By the war's end 65 million troops had been mobilised, three empires destroyed, 20 million military and civilians had died, and 21 million had been wounded. One in every 28 of the population of France had been killed; one in 57 for the UK. The shock of such slaughter by seemingly civilised peoples caused Sigmund Freud for one to conclude that mankind was born with a 'death instinct'. The desire for death, he opined, was one of two powerful inbuilt instincts, the other being sex.

In the First World War, or 'Great War', around 80,000 British troops were diagnosed with what became known as 'shell shock', or what we now call post-traumatic stress disorder; 309 British and Commonwealth soldiers were executed by firing squad, mainly for cowardice or desertion (actually 266 for desertion, 18 for cowardice, although the difference would appear to be moot) – a very Lockean solution to the problem of forcing men to fight in the appalling slaughter of the trenches of the Western Front. Officers were armed with pistols, useless in war except at close range. But many thought them well suited to the task of urging their men from the trenches with the threat of instant retribution for malingerers. The French army in the field adopted even more draconian approaches. To preserve their discipline and their aggressive favoured strategy of *attaque à outrance,* in the face of the appalling losses suffered in August and September 1914, the French army established special *Conseils de Guerre* to try both officers and other ranks accused of dereliction of duty. The death sentence was the one usually handed down on those found guilty and there was no appeal. The sentence was required to be carried out within 24 hours and was awarded for offences which today would be found trifling. For lesser offences the

French persisted in the old system of 'penal companies' which were allocated the most challenging and dangerous tasks. When a whole regiment failed badly, its commander would sometimes resort to the ancient Roman legion's punishment of 'decimation' whereby men were selected from each company in a more or less arbitrary fashion and shot after a perfunctory court martial.

The rise of pacifism was another product of the death toll on the American continent and in Europe. The pacifist, however, who will not fight to defend others must take the guilt of seeing them die or the opprobrium of those who are prepared to make a stand. Accepting Socrates' doctrine that doing injustice is worse than suffering injustice, pacifists saw acting violently as worse than suffering violence; but to their fellow citizens they were merely cowards. Many tried to avoid this label by serving in non-combatant branches in the First World War, such as the Medical Corps.

There is also moral cowardice. Edmund Burke is reputed to have said, 'All that is necessary for the triumph of evil is that good men do nothing.' Turning away, pretending not to hear or see a situation which calls for intervention is by this definition cowardice, as is hiding behind bureaucracy or standing orders.

Can brave men also be cowards? Over time, exposure to the apocalypse of the trenches might sap the morale of an initially brave Great War soldier. Rear Admiral Sir Christopher Cradock, who died bravely and futilely at Coronel in 1914, wrote in his journal of 1900, 'all men hoped that they were not cowards and that I outwardly, whatever I may have felt inwardly, tried not to be an exception'.[1] German troops of the Second World War willingly followed orders of racial extermination which they surely cannot all have seen as right or just. Was this willing refusal to challenge authority and orders a particularly Teutonic aberration or just another manifestation of moral cowardice?

Up until the Great War, the practice of European warfare had been regarded as a largely chivalrous affair. Wars were usually sharp and short and, for the British at least, had involved fighting native tribal bands protecting their homelands from Imperialistic settlement with assegais and other primitive weaponry. The whole-sale slaughter of the First World War was unimaginable and sol-diering was seen as a suitable profession for the sons of the aristocracy, one in which they would behave with the courage and chivalry expected from their class. But the slaughter of 1914 made cowards of many men – the stay-at-homes who, seen on the streets of England in civilian clothes, would be given the white feathers of cowardice by a certain sort of lady (see Appendix 1). To be branded a coward meant social ruin; courage and bravery, sacrifice, *pro patria mori* were requirements of a good reputation in society circles. To be called craven, even by implication, was disaster.

This book is about the life of a man thought to be brave, and of great lineage who, for one instant's decision, was forever associated with an act that many saw as that of a coward. It possibly ruined his marriage; it certainly ended his career prospects; it forced him to be an exile from his homeland. That man was Ernest Troubridge and this is his story.

# *Dramatis Personae*

Where appropriate, the naval position they held on 6 August 1914 is given.

King George V of the United Kingdom
Rt Hon. H.H. Asquith, Prime Minister of Great Britain
Admiral Prince Louis of Battenberg, First Sea Lord
Admiral Sir Charles Beresford, MP, Admiral, retired
Rt Hon. W.S. Churchill, First Lord of the Admiralty
Rear Admiral Sir Christopher Cradock, commanding 4th Cruiser
  Squadron
Admiral Sir John (Jackie) Fisher, Baron Kilverstone, First Sea Lord,
  retired
Assistant Paymaster Henry Fitch, HMS *Defence*
Rear Admiral Sydney Freemantle, i/c Signals Division
Marguerite Radclyffe-Hall, writer
Paymaster Henry Horniman, Paymaster, HMS *Inflexible*
Crown Prince Aleksander Karageorge, Serbian Regent and Supreme
  Commander Serbian Army
Laura Hope (née Troubridge), sister to Ernest and Thomas
Rt Hon. Reginald MacKenna, Home Secretary
Admiral Sir Archibald Berkley Milne, CinC Mediterranean Fleet
Lesley Scott KC, MP, barrister
Vice Admiral Wilhelm Souchon, commanding German Mediter-
  ranean Squadron
Rear Admiral Ernest C.T. Troubridge, commanding 1st Cruiser
  Squadron, Mediterranean Fleet

Sir Thomas H. Troubridge, brother to Ernest
Lady Laura Troubridge (née Gurney), wife to Sir Thomas
Edith Troubridge (née Duffus), first wife to Ernest
Una Vincenzo Troubridge (née Taylor), artist, second wife to Ernest
Captain Fawcett Wray, Captain HMS *Defence* and Flag-Captain to
  Rear Admiral Troubridge
Admiral Sir Arthur Wilson VC, First Sea Lord, retired

# 1

## Heroes and Beginnings

Ernest Charles Thomas Troubridge was born on the 15th day of July 1862 in Hampstead, England, to Colonel Sir Thomas St Vincent Hope Troubridge, 3rd Baronet and Louisa Jane, née Gurney. Queen Victoria's reign was not yet half way through. Viscount Palmerston was Prime Minister. The American Civil War was over a year old. The Royal Navy had just launched its first iron-hulled, armour-plated ship, powered by a mixture of sail and steam. It was the apogee of the Victorian empire.

The name 'Ernest' comes from the Germanic word *ernst*, meaning bold, vigorous, resolute, and if courage and audacity are transmitted through genes then the baby boy would have inherited all those characteristics in abundance. His great grandfather was Sir Thomas Troubridge, the son of a London baker who rose to become an Admiral and Commissioner of the Admiralty, friend of Nelson (they served together as midshipmen in their first ship) and a member of his fabled 'band of brothers'. Nelson described him as 'the most meritorious sea officer of his standing in the service'[1] and Lord St Vincent stated that Troubridge had 'honour and courage as bright as his sword'[2]. He fought bravely at the battle of Cape St Vincent and with Nelson at the Battle of the Nile. Awarded a Baronetcy in 1799 for the retaking of Naples, where he again fought with Nelson (and a pension of £500 from a grateful King), he also served at the capture of Rome from the French, for which action he was given by the Pope the right to augment his coat of arms with the cross keys of St Peter.

Troubridge then served as a Lord Commissioner of the

Admiralty, in which position he fell out with his erstwhile friend Horatio over his inability or unwillingness to promote Nelson's favourites (and his disapproval of Nelson's increasingly public liaison with Emma Hamilton). Ousted by political manoeuvring he was eventually sent to command the East Indies Station and, after further in-fighting problems, was there drowned at sea off the coast of Mauritius when HMS *Blenheim* was lost with all hands in a cyclone in 1807.

His son, Edward Thomas, also served in the navy and attained flag rank, fighting with the fleet at the Battle of the Second Coalition and the war of 1812. But he found his niche in administration and held the posts of Fourth, Third and Second Sea Lord. He married Anna Maria, the daughter of Admiral Sir Alexander Forrester Inglis Cochrane and first cousin to Admiral Sir Thomas Cochrane, one of the most original and daring of British commanders in the history of the navy.

Alexander, son of the 8th Earl of Dundonald, fought in the Napoleonic Wars and in 1814 became CinC of the North America station and, eventually, Plymouth. A good enough pedigree for a sailor; but Thomas Cochrane, who became the 10th Earl, was in a different league. Known to the French as *Le Loup de Mer* (the sea-wolf) for his activities during the Napoleonic Wars, he was the model for the fictional heroes Horatio Hornblower and Jack Aubrey of *Master and Commander* fame. Thrown out of the navy for dirty dealing on the stock market, he became a highly successful and sought-after naval mercenary, fighting in the Chilean, Brazilian and Greek wars of independence. Reinstated into the Royal Navy in 1832, he reached the rank of Admiral and was made a Grand Commander of the Bath, dying in 1860 with the honorary rank of Rear Admiral of the United Kingdom.

Edward and Anna Maria had two sons. The younger joined the navy and died on the China station in 1850. The elder, Thomas St Vincent Hope Cochrane Troubridge (born in 1815) joined the army, the traditional career path for the eldest sons of the aristocracy, the blood of two martial families coursing through his veins.

2

Thomas was educated at Sandhurst College, purchased a commission as an ensign, served in several infantry regiments, inherited the baronetcy in 1852 as 3rd Baronet and as a major fought in the Crimean War. He was badly wounded at the Battle of Inkerman, fighting to defend the artillery batteries from the Russians, and lost his right leg and left foot. Refusing to leave the field until the enemy had been repulsed, he fought propped up against a gun carriage with his shattered limb leaning next to him. One Hugh McLoughlin, who served with the Major in the Crimea, wrote to his son of the bravery he observed: 'His noble courage, chivalrous devotion made under the greatest difficulty, in what must be his agony and pain, his wounds exposed to a piercing frosty wind – no bandages – …This valiant soldier who I am certain gave credit to every man under his command, none to himself.'[3] Lord Raglan, the British commander, observed in a despatch of 11 November 1854 that 'although desperately wounded he behaved with the utmost gallantry and composure'.[4]

His wounds were severe and given the standard of medical care and knowledge of the time he was lucky to survive them. Certainly they must have weakened his health and he returned to England, his fighting career over. But his bravery was respected and he received the Companion of the Bath (CB), was awarded the Turkish Fourth Class of the Mejidiye and the French *Légion d'honneur*. He was promoted to Colonel, appointed ADC to Queen Victoria and, eventually, given the post of Director General of Army Clothing, in which capacity he invented a new and better knapsack or valise for medical officers.

The returned hero was in need of a wife and in 1855 he married Louisa Jane Gurney, daughter of Daniel Gurney of Norfolk, at St Mary Abbots church, Kensington. Louisa must have brought a substantial settlement or dowry with her for the Gurneys were a rich banking family and Gurney's bank was a major private bank in East Anglia until it merged with Barclays in 1896. Daniel Gurney was a Quaker, antiquary, archaeologist and banker who established the West Norfolk and Lynn hospitals, was High Sheriff of Norfolk in

1853 and wrote books on his family genealogy, archaeology and several influential essays on the practice of banking. One of his sisters was Elizabeth Fry, the social reformer.

Daniel and his family were intimate with Edward, Prince of Wales, later King Edward VII, as the Sandringham estate was only some eight miles from the Gurney home at North Runcton and they often shot together. They also moved in artistic circles being intermarried with the Princeps of Little Holland House and through them mixed with such Victorian artist luminaries as G.F. Watts (who painted Colonel Sir Thomas) and Sir Edward Poynter. Thomas and Louisa quickly set about producing no fewer than three sons (of whom two survived) and four daughters and eventually established a family home in Park Street, Westminster. Ernest was their third son (see Appendix 2).

But tragedy was not far away. In 1867 Louisa died, aged only 36; and five weeks later, at 52 and no doubt weakened by his long-tolerated wounds, so did Thomas. They were buried next to each other at Hopton Church, near Yarmouth, and memorialised with the inscription 'They were lovely and pleasant in their lives and in their death they were not divided'. At the tender age of five, Ernest was an orphan. The valour and lineage of two glorious families, a tradition of heroism going back over 100 years, the distilled essence of the Troubridge and Cochrane heritage were vested in two small boys. The eldest would inherit the title. The youngest would have to find his own way in the world. If anyone was fitted to be a hero, surely it must be him.

On the death of both Ernest's parents, a singular misfortune even in those days, old Daniel Gurney stepped into the breach. The children were cared for at North Runcton, their mother's childhood home, by servants and governesses until seven years later both Ernest and his eldest brother, Thomas Herbert Cochrane, were sent to Wellington College in Berkshire as boarders (via schools in Lowestoft and Twyford's near Winchester). By now Ernest had grown into a very handsome child. His sister Laura described him at age eleven:

'He is simply lovely. He has dark brown, awfully thick clots of rather curly hair and very white skin, a lovely little nose, angelic mouth and awfully pretty shaped face – altogether the sort of face one longs to kiss.'[5] But she also added that he was frequently angry, spoiled and sulky with a tendency to flamboyance. Around this time he acquired the pet name that his family and close friends would call him by for the rest of his life, 'Zyp'.

Wellington College had been founded in 1853 by Queen Victoria as a national memorial to the Iron Duke who had died the previous year. It opened in 1859 under the Mastership of E.W. Benson (later the Archbishop of Canterbury) with the objective of supporting the children of deceased officers who had held commissions in the army or in the army of the East Indies Company (of which there was a plentiful supply thanks to the depredations of the Crimean conflict and the Indian wars of conquest). Housed in purpose-built buildings to the designs of John Shaw junior (who had also worked at Eton College) and who chose for Wellington a rather grand rococo style, apparently at the direction of Prince Albert, it also boasted a gothic chapel by George Gilbert Scott.

The growth of the public schools in the 1840s and 50s was one of the phenomena of the time. While the aristocracy went to Eton and Harrow, the aspiring middle class, anxious that their sons should be gentlemen, were eager to gain for them a similar education, and the likes of Rugby, Repton, Stowe, Winchester and Wellington were established in response to this demand. And education primarily meant the Classics, reflecting the Victorian obsession with Greek and Roman culture and role models.

The curriculum at Wellington, under Benson's successor, E.C. Wickham (a noted classicist), conformed to this format. According to the college year book of 1874, the education included: '1. What is usually understood by a good English and Classical education. 2. Mathematics. 3. French. 4. German. 5. Chemistry. 6. Drawing. These are arranged as follows. 1. For all – Classics (inc. History), Mathematics and French. ... with drawing and singing in the lower schools.' This was an adventurous set of topics in offering chemistry and with a mathematical focus too. Science was not generally considered a subject fit for a gentleman (reflected by the fact that only five boys chose to study it in the senior school that year).

Children could not be accepted before the age of 10 and between 10 and 12 were accepted into the preparatory schools on passing an exam. The cost per annum for qualifying 'foundationers' was £5, £10 or £15 depending on circumstances. A grant of £10 was made to the parent or guardian for books etc. Non-foundationers (i.e. those who did not meet the necessary military orphan qualification) paid £110 per year.

The elder Troubridge, Thomas – listed in the school records for the time as Sir Thomas Troubridge ma. (for 'major') – studied at Wellington between 1874 and 1878, becoming a prefect in his final year and showing some academic prowess, coming eighth in his class in his year of entry and winning a Form and a French prize. Troubridge mi. (minor), who entered into Combermere House (named for a distinguished officer under Wellington in the Peninsula Wars), seemed less well academically endowed, being sixteenth in a class of 25 for overall academic achievement, thirteenth in German, twelfth in French and sixth in Classics with a 'C' in both drawing and singing.[6]

Thomas Herbert eventually left Wellington for Sandhurst and an officer's commission in the 60th Rifles (King's Royal Rifle Corps). Younger brothers of the aristocracy either joined the church or the navy. Zyp, an athletic and good-looking child, was destined for the sea; in 1875, after only a year in college and at the age of thirteen, he packed up his travel chest and set off for the Royal Naval College, Dartmouth, otherwise known as HMS *Britannia*, a less academic and possibly more congenial environment. He could hardly have done anything else with the example of his ancestors before him.

# 2

## Cadet and Midshipman, 1874–1882

The Victorian navy was a gentleman's club; it was a yacht club for the aristocracy, a finishing school for the sons of royalty and a haven for those unchallenged by an excess of intellectualism.

Entry into *Britannia* required a nomination which was not easy unless one had connections. Every captain had a right of nomination on hoisting his pennant for the first time and the rest were under the personal control of the First Lord of the Admiralty. In this way the club membership was controlled. Candidates then had to take an entrance examination and a medical. There were specialist 'crammers' to get entrants up to the required level to pass the oral and written exams. The exam required candidates to amass a total of 720 points from a possible 1200. Subjects covered included 'arithmetic, as far as proportion and vulgar and decimal fractions', elementary algebra, 'up to easy fractions and simple equations', elementary geometry, Latin parsing and translation, French oral and translation and 'Scripture History'.

Ernest would have been a shoo-in for entry, his naval antecedents guaranteeing that he was 'the right sort' for admission. The cost of tuition was £35 a term, payable in advance, with a discount to £20 for deserving sons of RN officers. This was a substantial amount of money for the time and helped to limit the pool of available candidates to those of the required background.

*Britannia* was the fifth ship of that name, launched in 1860 as a screw ship of 131 guns. Two terms of cadets joined every year and each term spent two years on board. It was a tough and monastic life, exclusively male, with a regime of hard discipline and exercise.

The routine was dull and repetitive – prayers, inspection, classes, meals, boat work, exercise. After school there would be field sports. Punishments for misdemeanours included bread and water diets and standing facing the wall; it was a Spartan environment and an enclosed world with its own rules and culture, introspective, self-serving and self-absorbed. Cadets were not allowed to open accounts with 'tradesmen' or to have their own money over and above an allowance paid from their account by the Paymaster. Clothing and uniform had to be supplied by the cadets themselves and at their cost. The required articles included a hair mattress and pillow, six night-shirts and twelve pocket handkerchiefs!

*Britannia* was a sailing ship and Ernest had to master yards and stays, sails and masts, climbing and rigging. He was growing into a well-made young man and such physical activity no doubt delighted him.

The navy was stuck in a backward looking mind-set that refused to consider a changing world and looked to the past for its inspiration and training. The spirit of Nelson still loomed large. Still glorying in Nelson's tactics and ships, the service was resistant to change. Even when steam power was demonstrably proven to be superior to sail, the Admiralty hung on to masts and spars, and strange hybrid warships of sail and steam were built such as HMS *Inflexible* of 1881; she had 16-inch guns, 24 inches of armour, could steam at 15 knots and, uniquely at the time, had electric lights. But she also was fully rigged and as much attention was given to hoisting sails and taking reefs as Nelson or Jervis would have given.

In 1874 Captain Philip Colomb proved mathematically that carrying masts and sails round the world cost more coal than it saved, but old beliefs died hard; as did the adherence to old training regimes. In 1892 a Captain Johnstone presented a paper, which received wide support, in which he affirmed that 'I am certain that the only way of training sailors and men to be sailors is in masted ships, making them work the ships under sail, working the masts and yards, and entirely depending upon masts and sails.' There was no effort made to teach even the rudiments of steam – the syllabus would have been easily recognised by Nelson or by Troubridge's great-grandfather. As late as 1889 the Admiralty was building a sail training ship (HMS *Martin*). Such training continued until the end of 1899 when the remaining four sail training ships were decommissioned to release men for the Boer War, otherwise it could well have continued into the twentieth century. Admiral Gerard Noel, CinC Home Fleet in 1903, lecturing to the United Services Institute, deplored the passing of sail and masts and said that the new generation were no longer seamen.

The curriculum was divided into three parts – seamanship, study and out-study. While seamanship aimed to cover practical sailing sea lore and signalling, study gave the young cadets the chance to learn mathematics and navigation, with out-study focused on French and drawing (both very practical, France being our oldest enemy and an ability to draw maps and visualisations being of practical use).

Interestingly, naval history was studied at Oxford and Cambridge but not at *Britannia*. Much emphasis was placed on sports, especially sailing and boxing, and the ability to shin up and down masts and dress yards was much prized. These physical attributes were more likely to gain a cadet respect and progression than any academic achievement. Indeed it could be positively bad for one's reputation to perform too well in a scholastic manner. It was neither necessary nor desirable to be academically gifted in order to progress in the Victorian navy. Cleverness was regarded as suspicious and the furtherance of academic study was not encouraged. A 'three-oner' – a man who obtained first class passes at his Seamanship Board, Royal Naval College and Excellent (for gunnery) – was suspect, and 'three-oners' were held in contempt by many in the navy as being 'too clever by half', as were officers who pursued interests outside of the navy and sports. Fitting in socially, being a 'good sort' and coming from the 'right' background were much more important.

Despite missing the Easter 1876 term with erysipelas (St Anthony's fire – a streptococcal bacterial infection of the skin), which required him to be cared for at North Runcton Hall, Ernest performed well at *Britannia* and gained a first-class pass in seamanship with 930 marks. He passed out in summer 1877 (second in his class according to his own notes made later in life) to sail with the *Temeraire* on the Mediterranean station. Promotion from Cadet to Midshipman followed in October, having achieved at least 600 out of a possible 1000 marks available in topics such as 'ability to work a "day's work" by tables as well as by projection; to find the latitude by observation of the Meridian Altitude of the Sun, Moon and Stars; longitude by chronometer, and to work an amplitude'.

Troubridge was to serve on the *Temeraire* for five years. She was an unusual craft, typical of the confusion inherent in naval design of the time. Launched in 1875 she was brig-rigged ironclad with steam engines to supplement sail power. She was unique in that she carried her main armament partly in the traditional broadside battery and partly in barbettes on the upper deck. The design of the barbettes was itself unusual, being one of the few ships to have been equipped with disappearing guns. On firing, the recoil of the gun caused it to drop below deck level; this allowed re-loading without the exposure of the gun crew to enemy fire. After loading, the gun was rotated by a hydraulic system back into the firing position. While this system was effective, it was slow and expensive and was never repeated.

For a midshipman life continued to be spartan and tough. Living in the gun room with your peers, responsible for the ships boats, still supposed to study, a hard and energetic life as a 'snotty' which had to be endured for five years until a panel of four captains deemed you fit to progress to sub-lieutenant. The gun room was a tough place, bullying was frequent as were 'gun room evolutions' – roughhouse games, fighting and pranks – all ruled over by a sub-lieutenant or senior midshipman. Ernest would learn to use his fists and handle himself; as a well-built youth this probably did not present a problem.

*Temeraire* was based at Malta but in 1878 she was ordered to the eastern Mediterranean under the overall command of Admiral Sir Geoffrey Phipps Hornby. Hornby was considered a fine ship handler, a firm disciplinarian and something of a thinker. Quondam First Sea Lord Sir John Fisher wrote of him that he was 'the finest

Admiral afloat since Nelson'.[1] Russia's invasion of Turkish Bulgaria and the subsequent march on Constantinople meant Hornby was ordered to guard the Dardanelles, basing himself at Besika Bay and then Vourla. Here he suffered from the attitude of the British government which sent him puzzling and contradictory orders reflecting the difference of opinion between Disraeli and his foreign secretary Derby (incidentally Hornby's cousin). This saw the fleet ordered both in and out of the Dardanelles and the sea of Mamora before eventually anchoring (in part) off Constantinople. Ernest would have gained an insight into the age old navy tradition of 'hurry up and wait'.

As a lowly 'mid', Ernest would have no contact with such an august figure as Hornby but he would have been able to observe the great man at work from afar. He would also see the exercise of imperial blue water power, for the fleet had entered the Dardanelles after the agreement of the Treaty of San Stefano between Russia and Turkey, to which British Prime Minister Disraeli objected as, in creating the independent Principality of Bulgaria (in reality a Russian client state), it gave Russia too much influence in the Balkans and the Black Sea (as a result of this intervention, San Stefano was superseded by the Treaty of Berlin of the following year which gave two thirds of the principality back to the Turks).

Growing up at North Runcton had meant that proximity to royalty was not unfamiliar to Ernest and he had a further opportunity for close study of the species when in 1879 *Temeraire* and other vessels escorted the Duke and Duchess of Connaught (the Duke being Queen Victoria's third son) who sailed aboard the Royal Yacht *Osborne* for their honeymoon, in Italy. While there, Ernest took leave for the chance to visit Florence.

And then he took the first tentative steps on the road to a naval career. In October 1881 he was promoted to Sub-Lieutenant and, after a period of leave, posted to HMS *Excellent*, the navy's gunnery and torpedo school for instruction.

# 3

## The Lieutenant, 1882–1895

HMS *Excellent* was the nearest the navy of the time had to a graduate school. Officers went there to study gunnery, torpedoes, mines and elementary strategy. In conformity with the mores of the time, Troubridge did not demonstrate an excess of academic zeal or ability, gaining in 1882 a third-class pass overall, likewise in torpedo study but achieving a second-class pass in gunnery. Torpedoes were considered a sneaky and underhand technology so perhaps he was not too upset at his performance.

However, his adventures continued. Having seen the cradle of civilisation in the Med and Asia Minor he was posted in 1883 to the Pacific station to serve on HMS *Satellite* at the far flung limits of British influence. The Pacific station had responsibility for protecting trade and interests on the west coast of the Americas, based at Esquimalt, British Columbia, and the *Satellite* was a small composite sloop of 1,420 tons, later reclassified as a corvette, made of wood and iron, barque rigged with a small single-screw auxiliary engine and mounting eight 6-inch guns. She was ideal for trolling up and down the coast and showing the flag in remote harbours and inlets, but was not at the cutting edge of naval design even when she was built in 1881.

Returning to the UK, Ernest served for four months on the Royal Yacht *Victoria and Albert*, a formal gin palace of a paddle steamer (and the first ship he had served on without sails) where spit, polish and ceremony took precedence over any other considerations. It must have been a stultifying experience but one which carried the opportunity for making good contacts, for royalty were actively interested and involved in the navy and many a promotion was owed to royal influence.

Relief came quickly for on 3 September 1884 Troubridge was promoted to Lieutenant and found himself translated back to the Mediterranean on the battleship HMS *Agamemnon*, an ironclad turret ship armed with four 12.5-inch guns in two turrets. A noticeable quirk of her design was that she was almost impossible to steer and had a penchant for veering off in circles even with the helm amidships. It must have provided an interesting test for the watchkeepers, Ernest among them.

Fortunately, the navy did not consider the ability to fight as a high priority for the Mediterranean fleet. Complex drills, a pristinely clean ship and the enjoyment of the social life on Malta – opera, dances, picnics, polo, and horse racing – were the thing and a young officer of means and good appearance was a social asset and could have a very good time. The tall, handsome Troubridge no doubt did so. This happy sojourn lasted until December 1887 when he was recalled to England, but not before he had shown the bravery expected of a man of his descent by rescuing a drowning signalman, one William Davies, who had fallen overboard from a speeding torpedo boat in Suda Bay, on the north coast of Crete, for which, in 1888, Ernest was awarded the Royal Humane Society's silver medal and associated publicity and fame.

Ernest was clearly creating a good impression, for comments recorded in his naval record reflect credit on his performance. For example; 'promising' – Capt. Carpenter; 'most promising' – Capt. Nicholson; 'a zealous and able officer' – Capt. Long; 'I have a high opinion of his professional ability' – Capt. Rice.[1] It was not just his professional abilities that attracted attention. A fellow officer described him as 'the handsomest man in the Navy'[2], tall, strongly built and with a thick shock of hair.

Posted briefly to the outdated HMS *Sultan*, a centre battery ironclad attached to the Channel Fleet, in December 1888 he received the sort of appointment that young officers pray for and on which careers can be built – Flag-Lieutenant to Admiral Watson on the North American and West Indies station, a position Troubridge was to hold for five years and during which his life would change forever. An Admiral's Flag-Lieutenant was a key role, responsible for translating the flag officer's orders into signals to the fleet and generally running his communication needs. A good one was a blessing to any senior officer. A bad one could be disastrous (as Beatty and his Flag-Lieutenant were later to prove at Jutland and before between 1914 and 1916). Additionally, a Flag-Lieutenant was often expected to act as a sort of equerry and aide-de-camp to his Admiral.

Admiral Sir George Willes Watson was an old sea dog who had joined the navy in 1841 and had fought in China and the Crimea. Troubridge had served with him as a midshipman. Aged 61 at the time of his appointment, Watson had enjoyed a relatively conventional career, excepting that he had been accused of selling the cruiser CSS *Florida* to the Confederate navy during the American Civil War. This was to be his final posting before his retirement, and he no doubt looked forward to enjoying his appointment and the social life it offered, for the position came with a beautiful Queen Anne style mansion in Halifax, Nova Scotia, which was the fleet's summer station and an equally lovely house on the island of Bermuda, the naval yard of which provided the winter moorings. His wife and daughter Daisy went too (Watson also took 'two very fine horses and two thoroughbred cows'[3]) and his promising, heroic and handsome flag-lieutenant no doubt also looked forward to the pleasures of the station.

### The Party Years

Watson's flag-ship was the *Bellerophon*, commissioned in 1866. She was an ironclad battleship of some 7,550 tons. Fully ship rigged, she also carried one steam engine driving a shaft and propeller. A notoriously slow sailer, she could only manage 10 knots under full sail. For armament she was equipped with a central battery, originally carrying ten 9-inch muzzle-loading guns, replaced in 1885 by 8-inch breech loaders. Possessed of a variety of smaller calibres she also featured a weapon familiar to the ancient Phoenician sailors of yore: a ram! She had served on the North American station since 1881. In company was the *Pylades*, a 'Satellite' class composite sloop, also powered by sail and steam, dating from 1884 and armed with eight 6-inch breech loaders. By this time classified as a corvette, she had the distinction of being the last such built for the navy until the Second World War.

Neither of these vessels were at the cutting edge of naval architecture in 1889 (the British were building the 'Royal Sovereign' class in that year with 13.5-inch guns and fully steam powered) but martial considerations were far from Admiral Watson's mind; the purpose of the fleet was to show the flag and impress the locals with Britain's largesse. It was a social cruise, a whirl of balls and dinners, games and junkets. It was the apogee of the British Empire

Ernest, in company with Watson's suite, sailed from England to Bermuda on the SS *Orinoco*, arriving 24 January 1889 and promptly being entertained on the visiting German ship, SMS *Nixe*. March saw a concert at Admiralty House where Ernest provided part of the entertainment by playing the guitar; and then to Halifax Nova Scotia in June where Park Cricket Club entertained the combined *Bellerophon* and *Pylades* cricket teams in a game. The navy lost badly, Ernest taking two catches but scoring a duck batting at number seven. Halifax Summer Races followed before the squadron sailed for Quebec in August where the navy once again lost at cricket to the locals but the officers were entertained to dinner and dancing at the 'Citadel' as guests of the Governor General of Canada, Lord Stanley of Preston (later the 16th Earl of Derby), by way of consolation.

From there, Ernest, Watson, and his wife and daughter went to visit Niagara Falls in September, where they dined at the Clifton House Restaurant, returning for a ball given by the good citizens of Quebec in Admiral Watson's honour. The grand tour then moved on to Montreal (where they had to transfer to the *Pylades* as the flagship was too large for the river) and New York (where Ernest stayed at the 5th Avenue Hotel, Madison Square). Finally Christmas found them back on Bermuda.

The party atmosphere continued in 1890, which dawned with a pantomime – 'Bluebeard' – given under the joint patronage of Watson and Governor General Sendall before sailing to Barbados. Here the squadron staged a regatta before a ball on 7 February (by subscription) in honour of the admiral and the officers of the squadron, which was the culmination of a week of festivities including cricket (Ernest not selected and the game rained off), polo and three tennis matches ('there will be balls and parties galore' according to the local newspaper). Next, March found them in Jamaica and a joint regatta with the Royal Jamaica Yacht Club.

Then to St John's, Newfoundland, in July and a very different sort of reception. The locals were not well disposed to Watson or the navy for, under instruction, Captain Sir Baldwin Walker of HMS *Emerald* had acted to allow the French access to facilities and fishing grounds that the Newfoundlanders thought were theirs alone. Watson was seen as favouring the French and there was a great deal of agitation in the press. Many thought that they should not welcome the admiral with the proposed ball and the Chamber of Commerce refused to present the squadron with the traditional illuminated address. Eventually the ball did take place but the press was hostile and the atmosphere poisonous.

The point at issue was the 'French Shore', resulting from the Peace of Utrecht (1713). The treaty allowed the French to fish along the Newfoundland coast between Cape St John and Cape Ray, however it made no claims as to whether this was an exclusive right. As a result, France and England roughly shared the fishing grounds under an unstable joint sovereignty understanding. When the Newfoundlanders attempted to eject the French, Watson ordered Walker to enforce the treaty provisions.

August added even more prestige to the squadron for they were joined by HMS *Thrush* – itself a small vessel of limited utility; but its commander was Lieutenant Prince George of Wales, son of Prince Edward, heir to the throne of England and grandson of Queen

Victoria. The social cachet of the squadron rose several notches. And, for Ernest, it was to later prove the beginning of a long and prestigious friendship.

August was also the month that the ships sailed to Newport, USA. American society loved royalty and hopes were high that Prince George would be of the party but he preferred the quiet and seclusion of Nova Scotia and stayed away. Nonetheless, the New York Yacht Squadron sailed out in force to Rhode Island and there were weeks of parties and dancing. A Grand Ball at the Casino greeted Watson and his men, and there was fox hunting (using drags) too. Watson and Ernest visited the Vanderbilts and the local press headlined, 'This has really been Gala Week in Newport'. Watson was asked by the local press how he liked the 'American girl'. His reply showed tact and humour; 'I think she is tip-top. I am not doing any flirting at my time of life but I think she would be an awfully nice girl to flirt with.'[4] Not all was sweetness and light, however. Thirteen sailors deserted the *Bellerophon*. They were swiftly recaptured and put in irons.

The company returned to Montreal on 11 September and the citizens held another ball at the Windsor Hotel 'in honour of HRH Prince George of Wales, Admiral Watson and the Officers of the Fleet'. November found the ships back in Halifax where a thirteen-course dinner at the Halifax Club was held in George's honour.

All this time Ernest was learning the talents of a diplomat. It was an education in dealing with egos, VIPs and society figures. His childhood in North Runcton, among the wealthy, well connected and influential Gurneys, where a handsome and well-built lad would no doubt have attracted favourable attention from visitors, surely equipped him well for such tasks.

His education continued in 1891. The New Year was celebrated with an amateur concert in aid of the widows and orphans of HMS *Serpent* (sunk in November 1890 off the coast of Spain with all hands, 170 men lost), the navy all over the world pulling together to support its own. Then back to the Caribbean for the Jamaican International Exhibition, opened by Prince George on 27 January and a concert at the Court House in Port Royal where the star attraction was Miss Mamie Morris, 'the Denville Nightingale and the Coloured Jenny Lind of the United States'. Next Barbados, where Ernest collected the autograph of King Ja Ja of the Opoba tribe (in modern Nigeria), who had petitioned Admiral Watson to obtain his release as he claimed he was being held as a political prisoner on Barbados (he was released that year but died en route back to his homeland). Ernest kept the autograph in his scrapbook. During the same visit Prince George presented Colours to the 2nd Battalion Yorks and Lancaster regiment.

But it was not all beer and skittles. In an undated letter from the *Thrush* George complains to Ernest that he is disappointed that polo is cancelled for the day because of a dance. 'What am I to do today? I don't want to go to the general's dance and I don't want to go to your dance. ... D..n everything. I just feel like that.'[5]

April saw more amateur theatre with a 'Dramatic Entertainment' which billed Ernest playing a solo on the guitar during the interval (proceeds to the Seaman's and Mariners Home, Devonport). Troubridge clearly had musical abilities and was not afraid to display them. And as 1891 – and the posting of Watson and Troubridge – drew to a close, Halifax again and an 'At Home' thrown by Lt-Col. Curzon and the officers of the Halifax brigade garrison at the Halifax Hotel.

Such was the life of an officer in the British navy of the end of the nineteenth century. Social, dancing and musical skills were essential, as was a good digestion. 'Good chaps' were prized. As to fighting ability, it was simply assumed to be there. This was the milieu in which Ernest's maturing character was developed. His reputation is burgeoning, his network extending, his social skills evolving; but he has done nothing to indicate the presence yet of any martial qualities.

## Edith

The travel and whirl of dances and dinners did not occupy all of Ernest's time, for during his service on Nova Scotia he met Edith Mary Duffus, daughter of William ('the prettiest girl on the island' according to his sister-in-law Laura).[6] The Duffus family were wealthy merchants, descended from one William Duffus of Banff, Aberdeenshire who had emigrated to Nova Scotia in 1784, aged twenty-two. In 1815 his daughter Susan married Samuel Cunard, who went on to found the famous Cunard Lines steamship company. Ernest must have met Edith early in his posting for, at a Naval ball in Halifax of 1890, his dance card records that out of 13 dances he danced with her four times – two polkas, the Lancers and a valse – and once with her mother (and twice with Lady Walker, wife of Sir Baldwin, captain of HMS *Emerald*).

And so it was that on 29 December 1891, at the end of his posting and as Watson hauled down his flag for the last time, Ernest and Edith were married at St Luke's Cathedral, Halifax. Edith had been unwell in the weeks leading up to the ceremony but on the day she looked radiant. The church was still bedecked with Christmas decorations. The bride wore a cream and white striped brocade with a design of palm leaves and roses, and a veil of plain white tulle fastened with pearl pins. The best man was (army) lieutenant MacGowan, resplendent in his full dress uniform. Ernest wore 'best undress'. The bride's mother wore tweed!

The *Halifax Globe* newspaper of 29 December reported the wedding thus: 'At St Luke's Cathedral this morning a fashionable wedding which has been looked forward to with interest was solemnised. The principals in the event were Flag Lieutenant Trowbridge [sic] of HMS *Bellerophon* and Miss Edith Duffus, daughter of William Duffus. The bride was considered the Belle of Halifax. The groom is an exceedingly popular officer.' The wedding gifts included a large beaten silver punch bowl and some 'exquisite' fans, the latter from the best man.

The couple left for their honeymoon in Montreal where they

stayed at the Windsor Hotel. The bill for their stay was $123. And then Ernest returned to his ship for passage to England and Edith followed at a more leisurely pace by passenger liner, via New York. They were both twenty-nine, both attractive. Hers was a late age to marry (the median woman's age at marriage in 1891 was 23.6 in England and 22 in the USA). Had Edith been saving herself for a better catch than she could find on her home turf? The population of Nova Scotia in 1891 was only 450,396, of which 71,358 were in Halifax. Was she bowled over by the handsome, dashing lieutenant? Was it a love match or did Ernest win her hand because she could see no better prospect?

That, for Ernest at least, it was a love match can best be surmised by his speech at a dinner given in his honour by the Halifax Whist Club. Thomas Kenny MP, in his speech of welcome, joshingly accused Ernest of 'capturing one of the fairest daughters of our city'. In a reply considered surprising for its high standard of oratory, Troubridge said, 'I really must beg leave to traverse [*sic*] that statement. Let me, gentlemen, with more modesty, put it this way; that I came among you, and after a very short time and with hardly a parley, I surrendered unconditionally and at discretion. I came, I saw and I was conquered.'[7] Prince George, recovering from typhus at Sandringham, wrote, 'I don't know which day you did marry but allow me to wish you both every possible luck and happiness in the future,'[8] and wished them a delightful honeymoon.

As well as providing him with a wife, the station had professionally advanced Ernest's career. His work had clearly satisfied his superiors. Old Admiral Watson formally described him as an 'excellent signals officer'; and Captain Gissing, at the end of Troubridge's time on the station, proposed him for advancement: 'works well with the ship's company and recommended for promotion'.[9]

But that much wished-for sublimation was still some way off. Back in Britain, in May 1892, Ernest was posted to HMS *Volage*. He received a letter of congratulation from Prince George in which George asked to be remembered to Edith; he also sent a belated wedding present. *Volage* was one of the four ships – together with her sister ship *Active* and the *Ruby* and *Calypso* – which made up the Training Squadron that had been training up boys to be seamen since 1886. She was an iron screw corvette launched in 1867, ship rigged with a full set of sails and a two-cylinder steam engine driven by five boilers. She carried ten 6-inch 80-pounder breech-loading guns and two 14-inch torpedo tubes, and was obsolete when launched and an anachronism now. Around 350 boys and officers served on her, learning the intricacies of cleaning ship, dressing yards, weighing anchor, firing the antique guns and polishing anything that didn't move (and much that did). Ernest had become a naval schoolteacher.

In 1893 he had the pleasure of attending his brother's wedding. Thomas Herbert had inherited the baronetcy at the age of seven and had served ten years with the 60th Rifles ('that cradle of good soldiers and good fellows').[10] In common with other Rifle Regiments the 60th Rifles (Kings Royal Rifle Corps) considered itself an elite unit, not least because – as with the other rifle formations – it was a 'black button' outfit (allowed to wear black rather than shiny uniform buttons) which carried a certain cachet. The 'black button mafia', as the regiments were known had a degree of prestige and produced a number of the bigger army names in the First World War including Field Marshall Sir Henry Wilson and General Sir Henry Rawlinson. Thomas Herbert married Laura Gurney, daughter of Daniel Gurney's son Charles, at Christ Church, Down Street, London. The bride was given away by the Earl of Dudley. Among their wedding gifts was a £100 note from Edward, Prince of Wales; Laura had never seen one before. The Duke of Fife (Edward's son-in-law) gave a diamond bracelet. The Countess of Dudley hosted the wedding breakfast at Dudley House in Park Lane. Both brothers had now started family life (see also Appendix 3). In the same year Ernest's sister Violet also married into the Gurney dynasty, becoming the wife of Walter, the son of Somerville Gurney

The training squadron was based in Chatham or Portsmouth (the Troubridges set up house at 15 Cavendish Road, Southsea) so

Ernest would have had lots of opportunity to see his new wife – and his brother's family – during this three-year assignment. In February 1894 Edith presented him with a daughter, Mary Laura, and in the same month of 1895 with the much wished for first son, Thomas Hope (another daughter, Charlotte Edith, was to follow in 1896). But this newfound domestic bliss did not seem to affect Ernest's professional development for he continued to impress his superiors. Signal N2980/95, a letter from his captain, forwarded and endorsed by the flag officer in charge of the squadron, strongly recommended him for advancement.

The bonds forged in the three-year cruise of the *Bellerophon* were clearly strong, for in May 1894 and 1895 Ernest attended the 'Old Ship Dinner' in memory of the time. The menus show that ten courses were provided at the first of these but only six at the second.

May 1895 also saw Troubridge paid off from *Volage* and he went to HMS *Excellent* to take an advanced gunnery course, obtaining a second-class pass. In June he was promoted to the rank of Commander; and in July his erstwhile flag officer in the Training Squadron, Commodore Second Class Robert Hastings Harris, was promoted to Rear Admiral and Second in Command, Mediterranean Fleet. And Ernest was appointed to serve on his flag-ship in the most prestigious station in the British navy. Surely Troubridge must have felt that 1895 was something of an *annus mirabilis*.

# 4

## *The Commander, 1895–1901*

The naval rank of Commander (roughly equivalent to Lieutenant-Colonel in the army) is a pivotal one, both in terms of the role on board ship and in career development. A commander might actually command a smaller craft; on larger warships he was responsible for presenting the ship to the captain as a smoothly functioning and well trained weapon, to be deployed as the captain saw fit. It was the equivalent of a modern chief operating officer in a larger commercial business. A quondam First Sea Lord wrote of the role, 'there is no greater test of character in the world than to be the executive officer [commander] of a big ship'.[1] And in career terms it was an essential step towards the post of captain, from which the attainment of flag rank was almost guaranteed. Serving on the Admiral's ship, as second in command to his Flag-captain, was an excellent shop window for a man ambitious of further promotion; and Malta was an excellent base from which to demonstrate social and societal skills as well.

It was also the pre-eminent command in the British navy – and one that carried attendant risk in time of war. Of the Mediterranean Fleet, Admiral Sir John Fisher wrote in 1899, 'I don't like the Mediterranean! However, there's no mistake about it that the Mediterranean is the tip-top appointment of the Service, and, of course, if there's war, there's a peerage or Westminster Abbey. But it's pretty sure to be Westminster Abbey.'[2] Rear Admiral Harris's flag-ship was HMS *Revenge*, a Royal Sovereign class battleship launched in 1892, designed by Sir William White and one of the most potent battleships in the world until HMS *Dreadnought* rendered her and her sisters obsolete overnight in 1906. In their day the Royal Sovereigns embodied revolutionary improvements in firepower, armour and speed. The main armament of four 13.5-inch guns was housed in two barbettes, rather than turrets, at either end of the ship, which allowed a higher freeboard, greatly increasing their capacity for fighting in rough weather. However they rather made up for their advanced modernity by rolling like a pig in anything but a calm sea. The secondary armament of ten 6-inch quickfirers was designed to provide support for the main battery. Despite their greatly increased weight, resultant from a main armour belt which ran for two thirds of their length, they were the fastest capital ships in the world in their time. It was the first truly modern ship on which Troubridge had ever served.

He saw little action, however. *Revenge*'s daily routine was seldom disturbed by martial considerations, although from February 1897 through to December 1898 she served in the International Squadron blockading Crete during the Greco-Turkish uprising there, protecting British interests and citizens as the Greeks fought for their freedom from the Ottoman yoke. The squadron also held at least one concert party where Ernest's skills on the guitar were combined with those of a Lieutenant Humphrey on the Zither.

In 1898 Harris departed to command the South Africa station and was replaced by Rear Admiral Sir Gerard Noel. Troubridge remained with the ship. Admiral Harris was to play a significant role in the imminent Boer Wars, organising a naval brigade to assist in the relief of Ladysmith. But Ernest remained in the Med, with no opportunity to demonstrate any of his ancestor's courage and valour, although Noel did lead a British naval fleet to Candia to force the capitulation and disarmament of a Turkish garrison (who had massacred a number of Christians in a British camp on the Cretan island), land marines to form an occupying unit and to achieve the handover to British officials of the ringleaders of the outrage. A number of newly delivered and pregnant women were evacuated to the *Revenge* and their progeny, coming all together, overwhelmed the ship's medical department's ability to cope; Captain Reginald

Prothero, universally known as 'Prothero the Bad', called for volunteers from the crew to support them and in the end there arose a great competition between the sailors messes to see who had the cleanest baby! Captain Prothero, huge, black bearded, hook nosed and a difficult man to please, wrote of Troubridge at the time, 'Great tact and judgement in handling large bodies of men and very even temperament.'[3]

In the Victorian British navy the acme of all that was prized was to be found in the Mediterranean fleet. Based at Malta, sunny, cheap, far away from the travails of home, it was a posting much to be wished for. Ernest eventually enjoyed several appointments to the island. The Med was Britain's *mare nostrum*, a playground for its rich and for its navy. Here officers could live the life they lived at home, enjoying the privileges of their class, but at lower cost

The social life was superb. Admiral C.C. Penrose Fitzgerald, writing in his autobiography of his service in the Med in 1889, emphasised it: 'Very good opera companies used to come to Malta for the winter months. ... then, it was extremely cheap – two-and-six for a stall and boxes in proportion. Several stars, including Albani, made their debut at the Malta Opera House. There were balls, parties, picnics, polo, gymkhanas, and golf. Many of the officers of the Mediterranean squadron got their wives out from England for three or four of the winter months, and as these frequently brought with them other ladies, there were plenty of dances, riding picnics, and other innocent relaxations from the stern routine of naval discipline. The great event of the season was the fancy-dress ball at the Governor's palace. The various and picturesque costumes of the East were always well represented ...'[4]

One of the few drawbacks of life on Malta was the prevalence of 'Malta Fever', an unknown infection at the time, now recognised as brucellosis. Malta fever was a killer and a constant worry for commanding officers hoping to keep their men at a high pitch of fitness. Between 1898 and 1906 a yearly average of 348 sailors were diagnosed with the fever, of whom an annual 180 were subsequently invalided out of the service and 6 per year died. The disease was not conquered until the end of the first decade of the twentieth century when, on 14 June 1905, Maltese doctor Themistocles Zammit found that five out of six goats reacted to the blood test for what was eventually isolated as brucellosis. He was able to prove a link to goat's milk from apparently healthy goats, the infection then spreading through milk products, as an aerosol from infectees, and occasionally by mosquitos which had fed on the goat's blood. In recognition of his efforts, Zammit was later knighted.

Meanwhile, the fleet cruised up and down, its programme largely social and its practices largely based around complex and centralised 'evolutions' – manoeuvres. These choreographed routines were like an army parade-ground display and bore little or no resemblance to the likely needs of a shooting war. When ashore, officers could enjoy dinner parties, fancy dress balls, shooting, regattas, tennis parties, golf, cricket; and if you had the financial resource, polo and horse racing. Zyp played tennis and golf regularly. A generation of future flag officers grew up in this comfortable environment. Military 'bull' was the rule, a smart and clean ship the route to promotion, following orders and 'fitting in' socially the most important aspect of behaviour.

And keeping a smart ship was primarily the commander's role. Admiral's inspections focused on the appearance of both men and ship. There were regulations covering, *inter alia*, all aspects of permissible dress for men and officers (up to and including the length of the men's trouser legs) and the length and type of beards (the ship's captain's approval was necessary both to grow one and to shave it off, and only a 'full set' was allowed). Regular sporting activities were arranged between the ships of the fleet, particularly rowing regattas and captains thought it important that their crews should be both victorious and smartly turned out.

As for the ship itself, it had to positively gleam and sparkle in the Mediterranean sun. Commanders' desirous of promotion often paid from their own pockets to buy gold leaf, brass polish, extra brass fittings and paint to decorate their vessel. Gunnery practice was abhorred (and often ignored) as it made the ship dirty. Many captains, sent to fire off practice ammunition at sea, simply threw it overboard.

When at sea the fleet cruised in balletic formations, devised by the admiral. Absolute adherence to the admiral's plans was required and formation sailing was the rule. Orders were gospel and not to be questioned. The admiral knew best and initiative was completely discouraged. Captains followed orders religiously and likewise ship's officers followed their captain's orders without question.

While in the Med, Ernest was given some opportunity for independent command. Assigned briefly to command HMS *Shark* (a 'Rocket' class destroyer built in 1894 and armed with one gun and two torpedoes) in 1896 his vessel was inspected by Captain Burgess Weston who commented 'ship clean and efficient throughout'.[5] In January 1897 he was invalided home to the Royal Hospital Plymouth for 'an uncertain period' (probably having contracted 'Malta fever') but returned to his post in the same year. And then, in December 1899, triumph and disaster at the same time. A glowing report from Captain Briggs, his commanding officer, concluded that Ernest was an 'exceptionally good officer, recommended for promotion'; and he was granted leave to return to England because of 'the illness of his wife'.[6]

On 28 December the Troubridges' fourth child, Edgar Godfrey, was delivered stillborn. Edith, Zyp's beautiful wife of less than nine years, died of childbirth complications two weeks later. In January 1900 the devastated widower was left with three small children – aged five, four and three – to care for. He kept the handmade Christmas cards they had given him days before; the one from little Thomas stating in a round, large hand 'to daddy from Tommy'.

Among the letters of consolation he received, the one from Prince George must have meant much. 'I have only just learnt with great grief of your terrible loss. I know well all your dear wife meant to you and what a terrible blank must be left in your life . . . . [I] offer you my heartfelt sympathy . . . in your irreparable loss . . .'[7]

# 5

## *George, 1886–1891*

Ernest had had connections with royalty since his childhood. Edward VII was a friend of the Gurneys, Troubridge had served on the Royal Yacht, and he had visited Sandringham. Most importantly he had served with Prince George on the North American and West Indies Station. The future King, George's father, had given a gift at his brother Thomas's wedding. It was perhaps no surprise therefore that he gained a royal friendship.

George Frederick Ernest Albert, His Royal Highness Prince George of Wales, was born on 3 June 1865, the second son of Edward, Prince of Wales, and his wife Princess Alexandra. Edward, Queen Victoria's first-born son, had endured what he perceived to be a miserable childhood at the hands of his overbearing parents and he was determined – both by inclination and by a lack of any real parental feeling for them – that his sons would not suffer the same fate. In this he was thwarted by his mother who, shocked to find the young princes growing up spoiled and ill-disciplined, insisted that they be put under the care of a tutor of her choice (in 1872 Victoria had remarked 'they are such ill-bred, ill-trained children').

John Neale Dalton, Cambridge graduate and son of a clergyman, had been appointed a curate in the parish of Whippingham on the Isle of Wight in 1869. This was the same church as was attended by the royal family when staying at their summer home, Osborne, and Queen Victoria came to know and like Dalton and pressed him onto the somewhat unwilling Edward as instructor to her grandsons. George proved the more ready to be educated, while his brother Albert Victor, called Eddy by the family and second in line to the throne, was considered backward, lazy, and obtuse. As second son, George was expected to follow a career in the navy but because of concern regarding Eddy it was deemed unwise to separate him from his brother, as George was considered a good influence upon him.

So it was that in September 1877 George and Eddy joined the *Britannia*, aged twelve and thirteen respectively. Dalton accompanied them, sharing their cabin and continuing to act as their guardian as well as chaplain to the ship. Perhaps unsurprisingly, the princes (Eddy nicknamed 'Herring' and George 'Sprat') – the latter small and shy, the other considered stupid – were bullied by other cadets who resented their exalted status (and perhaps this reflected the unpopularity of the monarchy at this time) and privileged position within the strict regime on the ship. They were made to fag for senior boys, and George later said that 'other boys made a point of taking it out on us in the grounds that they'd never be able to do it again'.[1]

Both brothers passed out from *Britannia* as midshipmen in 1879 (with what connivance from the authorities is not revealed). Neither the navy nor their parents really knew what to do with them, so it was proposed that Eddy should attend a public school while George continued in the navy, but Dalton recommended that the brothers should remain together. Instead it was arranged that both princes and Dalton should sail on HMS *Bacchante* with a crew carefully selected to be a good influence on the boys. The captain, Lord Charles Scott, was a son of the Duke of Buccleuch, while his nephew the future 7th Duke was part of the crew. Dalton went too and, despite the navy's and their parents' intentions to the opposite, saw to it that the princes had very little contact with all but a specially selected set of the ship's company. *Bacchante* was part of a squadron put together for the purpose, the flag-ship of which included Prince Louis of Battenberg among its officers.

In a three-year cruise they sailed right around the world, calling at points of the British Empire along the way including the Med, Egypt, South Africa, Asia, Australia (where George became ill), Japan (where he gained a blue and red dragon tattoo on the arm) and Canada. On their return in 1882, Eddy was sent to Trinity College, Cambridge (where he was a spectacular disappointment) and George began his naval career. He was promoted Sub Lieutenant in 1884 and Lieutenant in 1885, attended the naval college HMS *Excellent* in the same year (and unsurprisingly obtained a third-class pass) and then served in the Mediterranean fleet on a succession of battleships, including HMS *Alexandra*, the flag-ship of his Uncle Alfred Duke of Edinburgh, CinC Mediterranean Fleet 1886–89. He also fell in love with Alfred's daughter Marie who, for a variety of reasons, rejected him, eventually marrying the heir to the Romanian throne (and inspiring one of Dorothy Parker's best aphorisms).[2] This was perhaps a lucky escape, had he but known it, for the Romanian royal family was to become known for its casual approach to recreational sex. King Ferdinand was a submissive husband and hopeless father of an unknown number of children ('a master of indiscriminate fornication') while Marie had many lovers whom she used as counsellors, bankers and confidants, particularly Prince Barbu Stirbey, who would briefly be prime minister in 1927, and who probably fathered at least two of Marie's children.

Service on the Royal Yacht *Osborne* followed for George, then more exams at *Excellent* before he was posted in 1890 to the North American Station as officer in charge of the gunboat HMS *Thrush*, a composite gunboat of sail and screw propulsion. In 1891 he was promoted to the rank of Commander. Finally, in 1892, he took command of the *Aeolus* class armoured cruiser *Melampus*, acting as coastguard ship off Kingston, Jamaica. He was happy in his life. He had a career, position and was far away from the court and its stultifying routine. Then his brother died of pneumonia.

George was now a potential heir to the throne. His naval career was over (apart from a brief huzzah as Captain commanding the Edgar class cruiser HMS *Crescent* for a few weeks in 1898); his rank would now be ceremonial only. Like it or not, he returned to court, and in 1901 his father became King Edward VII and George, first as Duke of Cornwall and York and then Prince of Wales and Earl of Chester, was next in line to the throne.

Troubridge's and George's careers had overlapped at least twice, in the Med between 1886 and 1887 and again on the North American station from 1890 to 1891. The shy, retiring, formal, small (10 stones in weight and 5 feet 6 inches tall), reserved George somehow became friends with the tall, handsome, urbane and confident Ernest, and they were regular correspondents for the next twenty years. It was a correspondence built on friendship, and a friendship which had clearly been fashioned on the North American Station and through Troubridge's support of George, a retiring and private man who disliked the public ceremonial incumbent upon his royal status. George's protected life and his sheltered cruise on *Bacchante* left him with 'few naval friends and no intimates of his own age'.[3] Ernest filled the gap.

After leaving the squadron in August 1891 George wrote to Troubridge (from the Royal Yacht *Osborne* en route Aberdeen), 'I can't thank you half enough my dear Troubridge for all you did for me while I was out there with you and I really don't know what I should have done without you, you helped me in so many ways. … I hope it will not be very long before we meet again.' He added, 'I hope Miss Duffus is very well, please remember me to her. I trust that in six months' time she will be Mrs Troubridge.' He also asked after 'Miss Daisy' (Watson) who has clearly made an impression on him.[4] Thirty-four years later he would have his equerry write to her on the death of her mother from Palermo where he was cruising on the royal yacht: 'My Dear Miss Watson, The King was very sorry to hear of the death of Lady Watson, and he desires me to send you a message of most sincere sympathy in your great loss. His Majesty can never forget the happy days he spent at Halifax and Bermuda with Lady Watson, the Admiral and yourself nor the Kindness and hospitality shown to him always by your Father and Mother. May I also for myself offer you my very true sympathy. Believe me dear Miss Watson Yrs. very sincerely Bryan Godfrey-Faussett.'

When George's life changed irrevocably on the death of his brother, Troubridge wrote in consolation. George's reply to his friend shows the depth of his despair: 'I am quite crushed by this heavy blow . . . All my life is now altered in one short moment. God give us strength to bear this heavy burden in silence and to say "Thy will be done" however hard it seems.'[5] He shared his innermost feelings with Ernest in a way which his nature and upbringing must have made difficult.

In May of 1892 George wrote that he was going down to Norfolk: 'I only wish that you were going to be there too.' On 30 August, from Hunstanton, he 'would be delighted if you and Mrs Troubridge would come to lunch with us tomorrow or Sunday whichever suits you best at 1.30.'[6] And in 1895, on the birth of George's second son Albert, he wrote to Ernest thanking him for his congratulations and adding that 'no doubt he will join the navy, the profession that we both love so well.'[7] His letters start 'My dear Troubridge' or 'my dear Old Troubridge'; they end 'Your sincere friend', 'Believe me your sincere friend', or 'Believe me most sincerely yours'.

They were friends. And this tells something of Troubridge too. Older by three years, physically bigger and stronger, psychologically more extrovert and confident, Ernest provided a bulwark for George to hide behind and lean upon (the poet Henry Newbolt found George most uncharismatic; 'such a queer, shy, abrupt moving and small headed person').[8] To the orphaned Troubridge, a second son with no title and scant means, a royal friendship could be an entrée to a better world; and it reinforced his view of himself. Connected to royalty, close to the throne and power, a coming man, a man of substance and influence. A man who walked with kings.

# 6

## Japan and Return to the Med, 1901–1908

After Edith's sudden death, and with support from friends such as George and his family, who stepped in as the Gurneys had on the occasion of his own parents' death, Ernest was able to submerge his grief in his work. His spinster sisters Helen and Amy took over *in locus parentis* and Troubridge returned to sea with the Channel Squadron at Gibraltar, taking command of the third-class cruiser HMS *Pelorous* (described by one source as 'the unspeakably useless *Pelorous* class'),[1] just over 2,000 tons and with a crew of 250. Inspected by Captain Russell in February 1901, he received the glowing endorsement 'ship in all respects very clean and in good order'.[2] It should be noted that, as was normal for the times, no mention was made of any ability it might have had to fight! Finally, on 30 June 1901, Ernest received the promotion that he (and any other naval officer) craved for; he was promoted to the rank of captain.

To be a captain afloat was to be a sort of demi-god. Able to come and go as you please, in sole authority over hundreds of men, a secretary and personal servants, a private cabin and dining arrangements – it was a position of immense privilege and power. A captain came aboard his ship to the shrill, quavering notes of the boatswain's pipe. Marine guards snapped to the 'present'; officers uncovered heads. A marine sentry guarded his suite, which often contained the only proper bath on board. He was not addressed until he made the first approach. He had power and dominion over advancement and discipline; he was a benign (or otherwise) despot.

But there were more captains than ships needing them, and Troubridge was instead given a different appointment and one that suited his genial and socially adept personality – he was sent on diplomatic duties. Initially and very briefly sent to Madrid and Vienna, on 18 September 1901 he was appointed Naval Attaché to the British Embassy in Japan, based in Tokyo, where he was to serve for the next three years. We may speculate how the Japanese perceived him at first sight. The tall, attractive, shock-haired and imposing Troubridge would have seemed very alien to them; he stood out in all situations.

The Japan that greeted Ernest on his arrival was a country in the midst of rapid change. Since the advent of the Meiji dynasty in 1868, and the suppression and overthrow of the Tokugawa regime – the Shogunate – which had attempted to hermetically seal off Japan from the outside world to prevent change, the Meiji leaders had striven to pursue a new, westernised, course driven by the twin pressures of the Western threat to Japanese sovereignty and the need to revoke the unequal treaties imposed on Japan in the 1850s. Under the slogans of *fukoku kyohei* (enrich the country, strengthen the military) and *bunmeikaika* (civilisation and enlightenment), the Meiji government attempted to industrialise the nation and strengthen the army and navy to protect national independence. Their goal was to impress on the West that Japan was now an equal partner in world affairs and so could set its own trade tariffs and administer its own laws to Japanese and foreigners alike

This modernisation extended to every part of Japanese life. Government, and through it the army, were the first to make changes to clothing in Japanese society. A regulation of 1872 ordered the substitution of Western dress for the ceremonial robes of court nobles, and the Emperor had appeared in Western dress as early as 1870. Haircuts reflected the Westernising trend with the short cut replacing the topknot, so that by 1890 it was difficult to find a man in the cities with the old traditional hairstyle. For women, blackened teeth and shaved eyebrows began to disappear quickly from the cities and more slowly in the countryside. Western style hats and suits became commonplace as did umbrellas and pocket watches.

Eating habits also saw change with increases in the consumption of polished rice, tea, fruit, sugar and soy sauce. Dining out also became much more widespread and acceptable. Communications improvement and increased social mobility caused the spread of local customs such as the eating of seafood, which became an accepted part of the national diet. Meat eating was encouraged but did not immediately take off. Drinking beer did, however! First brewed in Japan in the 1870s, initially by foreigners in Yokohama, it soon became a popular tipple. The first beer hall was opened by Sapporo Beer in Tokyo in 1899.

Up until the end of the century, Japan's economy had been primarily based on agriculture and fishing. However, a change in the law which allowed land to become private property led to increases in agricultural productivity – but land was increasingly concentrated in fewer hands.

The Meiji regime also instituted a greater freedom in commerce, abolishing the guild monopolies and allowing the Samurai to engage in trade. The formation of joint stock companies and the idea of limited liability were introduced to Japan and provided new ways of accessing capital and participating in economic growth.

Modernisation had been fastest in the military – in terms of dress, technology and the hiring of foreign advisors. Conscription ensured the spread of new habits. Shoes, trousers, beds, tinned food, bread, beer and cigarettes gradually permeated into general society. The mixing of recruits from different areas and the conformity demanded by army life led to the breakdown of many local taboos and customs. And time quite literally changed, for in 1900 Japan adopted the Gregorian calendar. Even the very word for society – *shakai* – was a neologism. Japan in 1900 was on the fast track to change and hungry for Western acceptance – and Western input

As a result of this drive for industrialisation and militaristic rearmament successive Japanese governments had sought to modernise their army and saw, from Britain's example, the benefits of a blue water navy to ensure an ability to project power and protect trade. Accordingly, a 10-year naval build-up programme, under the slogan 'Perseverance and determination' (*Gashinshotan*), was put in place. The core of this 109-ship build-up was the 'Six-Six Program' of six battleships and six (eventually eight) armoured cruisers comparable to the British Cressy class.

Japan turned to the Prussian (and then German) army for help in modernising their military and to the British in order to train and build a navy. British naval officers were sent out to Japan for the purpose and the role of Naval Attaché was an important one in ensuring that British interests (such as obtaining the orders to build new ships for British shipbuilders) were furthered. With British help, Japan had thus built up a modern and well equipped navy by the early 1900s. The relationship between the two countries was further strengthened when in 1902 Britain and Japan signed an alliance, the first Japan had entered into. From the British perspective the treaty was intended to give her a reliable ally in the east against the growing power and imperial ambition of Russia. From Japan's perspective it was a display of her growing power and influence and a counter to Russia's increasing interest in areas that she thought were strategically threatening.

Troubridge was instrumental in building on the treaty of alliance to form a new relationship between the Japanese and British navies, using his presence and personality to become on excellent terms with the Vice-Minister for Marine, Rear Admiral Saito Makoto. Through Ernest's influence it was agreed with Admiral Sir Cyprian Bridge, CinC China Station, that under certain circumstances a British squadron would assemble in a Japanese port and cooperate with the Japanese navy. And Troubridge clearly saw this as a 'good thing' for he was effusive in his praise of the Japanese navy's performance in manoeuvres conducted in May 1903, at which he was an official observer, and he told Saito so. Then Troubridge became a witness to a war. The Russo-Japanese War of 1904–05, fought between Russia and Japan in Korea and Manchuria.

The proximate cause of the war was Russia's desire to obtain a warm-water port on the Pacific. She had long sought an ice-free, year-round port and desired control in part of China to achieve this.

Additionally Japan's expanding population needed territory, food, raw materials, and new markets; and both countries wanted control of Manchuria and Korea. In 1894–95 Japan's army won from China the Liaotung Peninsula, which juts out into the Yellow Sea between Korea and China. Russia, backed by Germany and France, forced Japan to return the peninsula to China, which caused much Japanese resentment. Then, in 1898, Russia took over the peninsula – including the ice-free port of Port Arthur. Technically Russia was only leasing the peninsula, but the presence of Russian troops and the extension of the Trans-Siberian Railway through Manchuria made it obvious that Russia intended to hold the area permanently. Russia was also extending its influence into Korea.

Japan objected to the Russian moves which it saw as imperialistic and counter to its own interests and, after unsuccessful negotiations, broke off relations on 6 February 1904. Two days later Japan commenced operations. In a shadowy harbinger of Pearl Harbor, they commenced hostilities without a declaration of war and attacked Russian warships without the customary preliminaries.

Troubridge and his colleague Arthur Ricado made strenuous efforts to get aboard the Japanese fleet as soon as they realised what was about to happen. The performance of the Japanese fleet – largely British built, designed or influenced – would give a good indication of how the (untested by war) British fleet might perform. For whatever reason, Ricado was not granted observer status but Troubridge was present when the opening shots of the war were fired at the Battle of Chemulpo Bay. (Also present – and moored in the bay – was the British cruiser HMS *Talbot*, under Captain Lewis Bayly. He resolutely refused to be drawn into any action against either side, but acted as a go-between for the Russians and after the battle he took on board many survivors of the *Varyag*, as service for which the Tsar later gave the ship's wardroom a silver model of a Viking ship, inlaid with precious stones.)

Here Troubridge saw the unopposed landing of Japanese troops and the attempted break out by the Russian ships in the harbour, the *Varyag* and the *Koreyetz*, the former being an American-built cruiser, launched in 1899. The Russians (under the command of Captain of the First Rank Vsevolod Rudnev) accepted a badly unequal battle, after Admiral Uriu gave the Russian ships in harbour a written ultimatum to sail by 12 noon or be attacked in the harbour itself. The Russians sortied but returned to harbour after battle having lost 31 men dead and 191 injured (out of 570), and eventually scuttled the ships. An American reporter described the scene at the time: 'Her decks were torn and riven and men were dashed down in mangled heaps for the guns had no shields to protect her crew. Like the furious wind squalls in the height of a hurricane came the bursting of terrible explosives all the length of the ship, shattering and burning and sweeping away men and pieces of machinery indiscriminately.'[3]

The devastation wrought by the modern Japanese weapons and the ease with which they destroyed the Russian cruiser were not lost on Troubridge. No one had observed the impact on human flesh and ships armour of modern weapons until now. The range at which firing was carried out also made a big impression on him. Both sides had engaged at long distances at a time when British gunnery prize practice, if carried out at all, was conducted at 3,000 yards. His sister-in-law later wrote that 'his reports excited great interest and much enhanced his reputation, both in our own and in the Japanese Navies.'[4] One such avid reader was King Edward VII, who annotated his copy of Ernest's report, 'I have never read a more detailed, exhaustive and interesting account with most valuable information for our navy. ... his services during the war are invaluable for the experience gained ...'[5] The hero of Suda Bay had further enhanced his standing.

Ernest's performance as an observer was a mixed bag. First he absented himself back to England in March as soon as he heard that Captain Pakenham was coming out to join him, despite the desire of the Admiralty to have two naval observers attached to the Japanese fleet. This was an odd performance. Rather than staying on, as did Pakenham, and taking the opportunity to observe further Japanese fighting, he left the country apparently believing – incorrectly – that he had been replaced with immediate effect.

Second, like the other attachés, both military and naval, he suffered from more general difficulties. First, Japanese culture made for secrecy. They did not want people watching 'their' war, even if for political reasons they had to put up with them. They were reluctant to tell them anything about the progress of events. While the British expected more favourable status than the other Western countries that sent observers, given the historic naval ties and treaty, the Japanese were worried about giving the impression that their war effort was being directed by the British. Their misgivings on this topic were exacerbated by tactless comments from Troubridge which later required Pakenham's efforts to smooth over, a service in which his friendship with Admiral Togo, the Japanese Naval Commander, no doubt assisted.

Such concerns would only be exacerbated by the press coverage resultant on Ernest's presence; a newspaper recorded ('from our St Petersburg correspondent') that 'all the papers give, in staring headlines, the report from the New York correspondent of a London newspaper that Captain Troubridge, the British Naval Attaché in Tokyo, is responsible for Admiral Togo's success, having planned the night attack on Port Arthur and being present at it in person.'

Ernest obviously took some 'stick' for not remaining in Japan, for Admiral Sir Cyprian Bridge, retiring from the China station, wrote in March that he 'admired your coolness and resolution. Your return to England to impress on the authorities the result of your experiences will in my opinion be of more benefit to the country and the service than you remaining [in Japan].'[6] Edward VII disagreed, commenting on Troubridge's return, he noted that it was 'a thousand pities'.[7]

Nonetheless, the Japanese must have appreciated Ernest's presence, for at the end of the war they decorated him with the Order of the Rising Sun and on returning home he received the Order of St Michael and St George. His seamless rise continued.

Back in the UK Ernest reported to HMS *President* for Admiralty duties and was assigned to accompany King Edward VII (and his entourage, which included Lord Selborne, First Lord of the Admiralty, Prince Louis of Battenberg, the noted pacifist Baron D'Estournelles de Constant, the Prince of Monaco and the Italian painter Chevalier de Martino, four cruisers and a flotilla of destroyers) on the occasion of his June state visit to Kiel, for which service the King invested him as a Member of the Royal Victorian Order (MVO). During the visit the King entertained his nephew the Kaiser, whom he detested, to lunch on board. Ernest was introduced to the Kaiser by Edward as having just returned from Japan. At this Kaiser Wilhelm yelled down the table to Troubridge, 'What impressions did you derive?' In the hush that followed Ernest calmly replied, 'I only derived one impression from it sir. The futility of a nation of soldiers taking on a nation of sailors.'[8] Edward was quietly delighted.

Next he returned to his favourite base of Malta. On 10 October he was appointed Captain of HMS *Victorious* and Flag-Captain to Admiral Sir Francis Bridgeman, second in command of the Mediterranean Fleet. Bridgeman had a good reputation as a ship handler and would in 1911 become First Sea Lord. Now he served under Sir Compton Domville who was superseded in 1905 by Admiral Lord Beresford.

Here Ernest gained further kudos when Queen Alexandra arrived for a state visit in the royal yacht *Victoria and Albert*; she was conveyed from the yacht in a state barge which sailed to the dockyard through an avenue of 24 fourteen-oared barges, all under Troubridge's command. The Queen was apparently impressed by the spectacle.

Troubridge and Bridgeman seemed to work well together (although there was a brief hiatus between June and October when Ernest was called upon to be assigned to the staff of Prince Arisugawa Takehito, the tenth head of a cadet branch of the Japanese Imperial Family, who was on a state visit to Europe); and when the Admiral shifted his flag to the *Glory* in October 1905, Troubridge went with him as his Flag-Captain. Certainly Bridgeman was moved to note in Ernest's naval record, in September 1905, the one word comment 'recommended'. Beresford was more fulsome in his praise. 'Zealous, good officer, sound physique, excellent judgement, considerable diplomatic experience, very enthusiastic, wants more practice handling fleet.'[9] If Charlie Beresford liked you he would praise you to the heights and the people he liked best of all were those who knew the social graces and old naval traditions. Admiral Sir Arthur Wilson VC, inspecting *Glory* in 1906, commented 'zealous and energetic with excellent tact and judgement'.[10]

Troubridge's intimate connection with the great and the good was extended in early 1906. The future Queen of Spain (Victoria Eugenie, granddaughter of Queen Victoria and first cousin to Prince George) wrote in February to thank him for his letter of congratulations on her engagement to Alphonso, the reigning King. She added a very personal note 'Cocky sends her love.'[11]

In 1907 Beresford was replaced as CinC by Admiral Sir Charles Drury (a Canadian-born officer and former Second Sea Lord) and Troubridge received the ultimate accolade for one of his rank – he was appointed Captain of HMS *Queen*, Flag-Captain to Drury and his Chief of Staff (Drury had been Flag-captain to Watson when Ernest was Flag Lieutenant; they therefore knew each other well. Drury wrote to Ernest, 'I am very pleased you have decided to come with me.')[12] Troubridge did not let Drury down. In battle practice his and his ship's efforts were sufficient for his record to be endorsed 'appreciation expressed' and in the same year Drury formally inspected the ship and noted that it was 'highly satisfactory'. And the King of Spain awarded him the Spanish Order of Naval Merit.

It was around this time that Troubridge, now aged 45, acquired the nickname by which he came to be known throughout the fleet. His thick brown hair did not recede with age; but it did turn completely silver-white. To his crew and the navy he became the 'Silver King'. (In so naming him, the sailors were probably influenced by the 1882 play *The Silver King* by Henry Arthur Jones and Henry Herman, which was one of the most popular melodramas of late Victorian England. It brought huge financial success for its authors and was eventually made into a film in 1929 by T. Hayes Hunter.)

*Queen* paid off at Devonport in December 1908 but before then Drury expressed his appreciation of his Flag-captain: 'In all respects a very fine officer with great ability and well fitted to occupy any high position that Their Lordships may select him for.'[13] Ernest, after nearly two years as Drury's right-hand man, got his reward. In the same month he was promoted to Commodore Second Class, in command of the Royal Naval Barracks, Chatham, and the final step on the path to gaining Flag rank himself. He was clearly a coming man with many influential supporters and a burgeoning reputation, especially for man management and tact.

But 1908 was memorable for him in a different way too – for on 10 October, at the British Consulate in Venice, he had remarried.

## Una

Una Vincenzo was born in 1887 to Harry and Minna Taylor. Harry was a Queen's Messenger in the Foreign Office, with the rank of Captain; his wife was related both to the minor Irish aristocracy and the Florentine family of Vincenzo and was believed by her family to have married beneath herself. Harry had been to Rugby School and Oxford University, subsequently joining the army which he left in 1883. He was tall, charming and handsome but also rather lazy, an amateur playwright, dissolute and lacking in ambition. Their child was christened Margot Elena Gertrude, but from birth was called Una, an ancient Irish name beloved of her mother. By some quirk, her birth was not to be registered for 46 years.

The family were genteel, but not rich enough to be comfortable or move in the circles that Minna thought their birthright. At a time when it was necessary to have an income of £600 per annum to support a carriage and two maids, the Taylors had Harry's salary of £400 and a large house, two children, a wife and several servants to pay for. There was no carriage. Una was often ill as a child but grew up with a precocious talent for drawing and design. Encouraged by her father, on whom she doted, she applied to the Royal College of Art in 1900 and passed the entrance exam aged only thirteen. In the same year she met and became friends with Jacqueline Hope, the daughter of Adrian and Laura Hope; Laura was Ernest's sister and the family lived in some style in Tite Street, Chelsea.

The Hopes were a well-off family with four servants and two daughters. Adrian was the son of Colonel William Hope, who won the Victoria Cross at the siege of Sebastopol in the Crimean War, and had worked in the city but was now Secretary to the Hospital for Sick Children, a position he held until his untimely death from appendicitis in 1904, aged only 46. He was also cousin to Constance Lloyd, the wife of Oscar Wilde (see Appendix 4). Laura worked as an artist and portrait painter. Her sitters included royalty, for in 1891 she had painted the Queen's sister and nieces at Osborne and met Prince George who wrote to Ernest that she was 'charming'. The reason for Una's attraction to the family is clear.

In 1905, while Troubridge was visiting his niece and family, Una was introduced to him. The 18-year-old budding artist was much taken by the naval captain, 'a handsome widower with three children' according to her diary.[14] From then on they continued to meet at Tite Street whenever he was home on leave. She found him 'manly' and he shared her (and his sister's) love of art. They all enjoyed music and the opera and Ernest liked to sing and play the banjo for her.

In 1907 Una's beloved father Harry died. Like Ernest he had been a big man with a shock of white hair; there was only eight years age difference between the two men. His death affected her deeply, and in the same year she was received into the Catholic Church. In 1908 Una and Ernest became engaged, he aged 46 with three children, she aged 21. It was said of her that 'young men did not interest her' and that 'she found maturity more attractive; she could trust it and it made her feel more secure'.[15] Some commented that she might be replacing her father. Indeed, Una was later to write, 'I met Captain Troubridge and married him chiefly, it must be admitted, because I discerned in his snow white hair and Terryish cast of countenance a likeness to the beloved and ever unattainable Scarlet Pimpernel of my dreams.'[16] There might have been financial considerations too – having endured a childhood of genteel poverty, with her mother constantly worried about how to 'launch her' into society, a man of prospects would be of interest. On promotion to Commodore in 1908, Ernest's salary was £1,095 per annum plus 'table money' of £185 10 shillings – more than enough for a carriage!

As for the Silver King, he would be flattered that a young, attractive woman, who was beginning to acquire a reputation as a sculptress of talent, found him desirable. He was a man of standing and lineage and had both sexual and dynastic needs. Ernest had a reputation for liking the ladies and since the death of his wife he had had 'escapades' with a number of women. Extravert and generally popular, 'his robust temperament and genial character made him friends wherever he went'.[17] Now he would have a sparkling showpiece on his arm, a living testament to his self-image.

After their engagement Una went to Italy to visit her relatives and see the sights. On her way back she called into Malta where Ernest was on station. Shortly afterwards they sailed to Venice and there married and honeymooned, at the Pension Chiodo Toffoli. The Silver King had taken a Queen.

# 7

## *The Navy in the 1900s; Fisher, Beresford and the Royals; Admirals*

The navy in which Troubridge grew up was a top-down, controlling, ordered world. All aspects of life were regulated and subject to routine. Orders were commandments. Admirals and captains were the benign (or otherwise) despots favoured by Plato. But for officers it also provided a life which paralleled the one they left behind and reflected the social class from which they were drawn. And it was as exclusive as a Guards regiment.

The navy was like a private club with strict criteria for membership, a sort of glorified yacht club for the aristocracy and landed gentry. Just as with a private members' club there were rules to keep out the riff-raff and promotion to the officer caste from the lower deck was strictly forbidden. The navy's ruling class was drawn from the same families as ruled the country at large and they fought hard to protect their privileges. As one titled lady remarked to an aspiring officer from the lower deck, 'the navy belongs to us and if you were to win the commissions you ask for it would be at the expense of our sons and nephews whose birthright it is'.

It was complacent, arrogant, sure of its own authority and greatness. To be an admiral or senior captain was to gain the publicity that is attendant on footballers today. *Vanity Fair* featured drawings of you. Newspapers wrote of your exploits and opinions. The tropes of the navy – dreadful sailor suits for children, full-set beards, smoking – became fashionable. Sailors and the navy featured in advertising for popular goods such as cigarettes and alcoholic drink. The Navy League had nearly a million members.

But this world of fame and society was not a united one, and to gain advancement Troubridge would have to be careful to play a political game. The Edwardian navy was riven with feuds. These fault lines split the Service, blighted careers, upset the natural camaraderie of the navy and made newspaper headlines. For into this cosy world had burst a man set on change and firm in his opinion that the navy had to modernise. The issue of the day was the reforming zeal of Admiral Fisher and the members of the 'Fishpond', his talent pool of handpicked supporters and acolytes.

Jackie Fisher (eventually Admiral of the Fleet Sir John Arbuthnot Fisher, First Baron Fisher of Kilverston) was the man who created the modern navy. Appointed First Sea Lord (and thus executive head of the navy) in 1904 he set about reshaping the Service. With the launch of HMS *Dreadnought* in 1906, the first all big gun battleship in the world, he produced the definitive capital ship rendering obsolete all others – including the ones in Britain's navy. His modernising enthusiasm changed training programmes for officers and men, introduced oil-fired engines and turbines, made engineer officer a respectable position and reconfigured the navy's forces. He recalled ships from far flung postings (and the admirals who commanded them), concentrated the navy where he expected it to have to fight (the Channel and the North Sea) and scrapped 150 ships (and, of course, the position of commanding them) deeming them 'too weak to fight and to slow to run away'.

Fisher was the son of a Ceylonese tea planter, from a poor background, a man who rose to high rank through ability not connections or his position in society. He was volcanic in temperament, Old Testament in expression, intolerant of fools or anyone who disagreed with him and a compulsive and skilful dancer. If he liked you he was easy to love. But he was also easy to hate, especially if you thought that he was ruining the traditions of the navy and reducing the power one held or one's opportunities for progression. One man hated him with a passion – Admiral Lord Charles Beresford.

Fisher's rift with Beresford probably has its genesis in an incident when Fisher commanded the Mediterranean fleet with Beresford as his number two. Beresford's flag-ship made a hash of anchoring on coming into port. Fisher signalled in public and *en clair*, 'your flag-ship is to proceed to sea and come in again in a seamanlike manner'. The pompous and self-important Beresford never forgave this public humiliation and the two men became sworn enemies.

Charles William de la Poer Beresford, Charlie B to his admirers, was a man of limited intellect, great snobbery, a family pedigree going back to the Norman Conquest, a large estate in Ireland and an MP to boot. Charlie B believed that he should have the top job and that Fisher was preventing it. He saw Fisher as an inferior and arriviste, while Fisher was jealous of Beresford's inherited wealth. Beresford did everything he could to destroy Fisher and his reforms, was a frequent 'leaker' to the press and used his position in par-liament to undermine Jackie which eventually led to a Cabinet Parliamentary enquiry. The war between these two outsized char-acters split the service and officers had to take sides. If you were one of Fisher's chosen few, Beresfordites would attack you, and vice versa. Fisher called the Beresfordites 'the Syndicate of Discontent'. The schism caused fault lines through the navy. A Fisherite serving under a Beresfordite would have limited chance of successful advancement, and vice versa.

Fisher was unsparing in his quest to modernise the navy: 'I'll alter it all, and those who get in my way had better watch out. I've ruined eight men in the last eighteen months and I'll ruin anyone who tries to stop me. I'd ruin my best friend if necessary for the service.'[1]

The feud was pursued with malevolent determination and it caused the ruin of more than a few careers and reputations. Beresford eventually was able to force a CID sub-committee review chaired by Prime Minister Asquith, and its half-hearted endorsement of Fisher caused him to resign his post in 1910. Many admirals and other senior figures had testified for and against the protagonists and this ensured that the fault lines continued even after the prin-cipal actors had departed the stage.

An example of the views held by the Beresfordite camp can be found in the writings of (then) Captain Christopher Cradock in his book *Whispers from the Fleet*, written in 1907 at the height of the Fisher reforms. 'We require – and quickly too – some strong Imperial body of men who will straightway choke the irrepressible utterings of a certain class of individuals who, to their shame, are endeavouring to break down the complete loyalty and good comradeship that now exists in the service between the officers and men; and who are also willing to commit the heinous crime of trifling with the sacred laws of naval discipline.'[2]

Fisher also fulminated against the influence of the King and his circle on appointments that he believed were in his purlieu alone, despite his own close friendship with Edward VII whom Fisher revered. The influence of the court on Admiralty appointments was considerable and often destructive. Service on the royal yachts was a proven route to promotion and favour as were royal connections. Edward VII and his son George V were both passionate about their navy and about sailing in general.

As one example, the choice of Fisher's own successor caused much friction with royalty. George V supported the claims of Admiral Hedworth Meux, a Beresford supporter (as was George who disliked Fisher, a feeling that was reciprocated), to be named First Sea Lord 1911. This was violently against Fisher's wishes. He was not chosen, as Fisher intrigued with Churchill against Meux. But under royal pressure Fisher was then thwarted, and the King pleased, as Meux was instead appointed to the prestigious post of Commander-in-Chief, Portsmouth.

The naming of ships was another prerogative which both kings arrogated to themselves. Churchill, when First Lord of the Admiralty (and hence responsible to Parliament for naval matters), had a series of running (and ill-chosen in reality) fights with George V over the naming of new capital ships (George disliked Churchill too).

So how did Troubridge navigate through these shoals of political complexity? Certainly he was well connected to royalty and particularly to George V when Duke of York. They had served together as lieutenants and were regular correspondents, as was seen in Chapter

5. But he does not seem to have adhered publicly to either the Fisher or Beresford camps, despite serving as Flag-captain to Admiral Drury when that officer was second in command of the Mediterranean Fleet under Beresford. Neither camp seems to have claimed him as their own, and his smooth progression through the ranks was uninterrupted by any antagonism.

That Ernest was able to operate on both sides of the Fisher–Beresford divide was a tribute to his tact (or to his ability to 'play the game') learned under old Admiral Watson, and is shown in his regular correspondence with both antagonists. He had served under Beresford in the Mediterranean between 1905 and 1907 and there is a body of correspondence between the two of them regarding manoeuvres and theoretical dispositions dating to 1905 and 1909. The Prince of Wales was in the Beresfordite camp and this must, of course, have accentuated Troubridge's acceptability to Charlie B.

But Fisher too sought Ernest's company and conversation. As early as May 1904, Fisher invited Ernest to Admiralty House, Portsmouth for the weekend: 'We lunch at two. I hope you will stay with us until Monday'.[3]

An interesting insight into both Fisher and Troubridge's personalities is given by an exchange of letters in May 1906, when Ernest is captain of the *Glory* (and Beresford the admiral commanding). Fisher had been buttonholed by the Prince of Wales who was concerned regarding the unrest caused by Fisher's breakneck programme of reform. Recognising Ernest's friendship with the Prince, Fisher (through his 'devil', Commander Crease), asked Troubridge to write a letter saying that all was well in the fleet but to address it to Crease so that it would not look as if Fisher had arranged the reply.

Ernest jumped onto a high horse made in equal parts of status consciousness and moral affront; to Crease he wrote: 'I am not in the habit of giving my opinions re Admiralty policy to my subordinate officers and do not propose to make an exception in your case.'[4] But, he went on, he would write personally to Fisher if so requested by Fisher himself. Such prickly demeanour gives an insight into his relationships with officers he did not have to respect.

In October 1910 Fisher invited Troubridge to stay at his country seat, Kilverstone Hall for the weekend: 'We have two intellects coming.' Two days later he wrote again, addressing Ernest as 'my beloved Troubridge'[5] and telling him to bring his golf clubs. The following month he thanked Ernest for his role in getting Fullerton (his son-in-law) a post on the *Triumph*. (Fullerton had also served under Ernest on HMS *Queen* in 1907.) Troubridge's star was set fair.

## Admirals

The German philosopher Max Weber believed that any governing group would secure its authority through 'charisma', a term he brought into popular usage. Literally the word means 'authority bestowed by God'. To be an admiral, commodore or captain on foreign service was to be possessed of charisma, with authority close to that bestowed by a deity.

A flag officer could have authority over thousands of men and millions of pounds of weaponry, and the life and death of both friend and enemy lay in his hands. He made and unmade careers from the lowest sailor to the highest-ranking subordinate. He was possessed of plenipotentiary powers, and abroad on service represented the monarch and government. In the far flung corners of the world, away from communication with London, flag officers made and unmade foreign policy. The flag officer was the Supreme Being wherever he went, so much so that Admiral 'Pompo' Heneage refused to kneel for divine service in his naval uniform as a British admiral did not recognise a superior; Pompo always changed into civvies for such events.

Flag officers had personal servants, their own barge and crew, a suite of officers to fulfil their every desire or order and untrammelled authority over their ships and captains. Their orders were unquestionable, divine writ, omniscient and omnipotent. And if no admiral was present then this mantle of power fell to a commodore or senior captain afloat. And, as has been written, they took more risk than other high-ranking military leaders: 'The limelight shines more fiercely on an admiral than on his contemporaries in other fighting services because he lives continuously among those he commands ... his duty in war is to lead the fleet in the forefront of battle.'[6]

It was a job not without its rewards and, when on service, one that paid quite well too. As Rear Admiral in 1911, Ernest's pay was £1,095 per annum. That equates to over £100,000 in today's money. If not required for service an officer could be placed on half pay but this was an occupational risk worth taking given the other joys of the role, for in addition to pay, flag officers received 'table money'. When travelling to their appointment they would, in 1913 for example, receive 30 shillings a day. On hoisting their flag, this was increased to (in Ernest's case) £1,642 per annum (at today's values, £152,000). From this a flag officer had to provide for the messing arrangements of his staff. Kings regulations and Admiralty Instructions (KRAIs) of 1913 made this clear: '1385. Table of Flag Officer, &c.–The table of the Flag Officer or Commodore of the First Class shall be considered as the regulated place for the daily entertainment of the Captain of the Fleet, Captain of the ship, Secretary and such officers composing the retinue of the Flag Officer or Commodore as he may think fit to receive, when he is actually resident on board. When the table of the Flag Officer or Commodore is not kept on board, those officers must make the necessary arrangements for messing, on their own account.'

He had also to provide for the copious entertainment he was expected to give when on service abroad with the intention of demonstrating the largesse and generosity of the British realm to the locals. Rear Admiral Cradock, on service in Mexico in 1913/14, complained in a letter to his friend De Chair that 'the many foreigners here afloat – let alone British subjects – have eaten nearly all my stores and drunk most of the champagne, hence my call of distress.'[7] When in Galveston on a diplomatic mission he held a dinner and dance for the local worthies and his stay there was such a success that the Texans offered to pay his expenses – an offer he declined, settling his bills from his 'private purse'.

Captains and commodores received similar benefits as KRAIs makes clear: '1387. Allowance to Commodore Second Class.–A Commodore of the Second Class shall, from the day of hoisting his broad pendant by order, to the day of striking it, be entitled to 10s. a day in addition to his table allowance and to his pay and command money as Captain; but if also appointed to the command of a station, or if in the actual command of a separate squadron, and not being in either case under the orders of any senior officer, he may, if so ordered by the Admiralty, while actually within the limits of his station or while holding such separate command, receive an allowance of £1 a day instead of 10s.'

Commanders-in-Chief on station had the use of splendid mansions maintained for the purpose. Old Admiral Watson's accommodation in Newfoundland and the Bahamas has already been noted. The Commanders-in-Chief of the three Home Ports had a retinue of naval servants to provide for them until 1907 when the Admiralty enabled them to hire their own servants 'in place of the naval domestics allowed' and instead paid them a commuted allowance of £500 per annum, made retrospective to 1904, and the same amount to their secretaries. No doubt this led to a better standard of dinner service. In 1912 these same officers lost the use of their private yachts (in reality small steam vessels) and again pocketed a £500 allowance in lieu. Flag officers and captains had a personal coxswain who looked after their barge and was in truth a factotum or 'devil'. These sailors would follow their officer from ship to ship and on retirement of the officer concerned often became his valet or other senior household servant.

Pomp and ceremony followed senior officers everywhere. Larger ships had their own bands, recruited from the Royal Marines, which would play at every opportunity, mess dinners, dances, entertainments, divine service – or simply because the officer in charge willed it. The admiralty bore the cost of this. KRAIs again: '1368. Naval Bands.–The whole of the naval band service forms part of the organisation of the Royal Marines. All usual instruments, with cases, band stands and other accessories, for a brass and reed ceremonial band, will be supplied free of charge to the officers in all ships and establishments allowed bands, together with music to the value of from £8 to £15, according to the size of the band, and the Admiralty will bear the expense of repairs, &c., due to fair wear and tear.'

Officers also received a 'stationery allowance' to enable them to provide such paperwork and forms as were necessary for the running of the ship or station – there was even an allowance to cover the cost of binding the ship's books.

Such unbridled power and lack of oversight led to eccentric behaviours which might not be tolerated in other workplaces. Some were harmless, some more outré; Kit Cradock was accompanied everywhere by a dog. His fox terrier was with him in his final days on the Falklands and met its death with him.

Vice Admiral George Henry Cherry also liked dogs, being devoted to his cocker spaniel, Rover. But his real eccentricity was his interpretation of KRAIs. At one time these laid down that the costs of apprehending leave breakers was to be borne by the culprit. Cherry would land whole patrols to search for missing men, with instructions to spare no expense hiring rickshaws, carriages or even elephants in their quest. Five officers who served with him for a whole commission had a medal, 'the Cherry Medal', struck in ironic appreciation of their forbearance. Eventually some 100 were struck and worn with pride. Admiral John Kelly liked to spice up General Drills (the Monday morning evolutions designed to set everybody up for the week) with eccentric requests. Once, having ordered all of his ships boats away he sent the signal 'send a poached egg to the flag ship'.

Robert Keith Arbuthnot was a martinet who once, as a commander, published a 300-page document of standing orders for his ship, when the norm called for two or three. He was a physical fitness and boxing fanatic and as a captain and admiral would randomly challenge members of his crew to a bout, which he always won. A keen motorcyclist, he kept his bike in his day cabin and raced it regularly. He exercised every day and insisted on a daily church service for the crew during which he would lecture them on the Christian virtues.

Jackie Fisher, the man who brought the modern British navy to life, loved to dance. He would dance anywhere and with anyone, regularly dragooning unsuspecting midshipmen into marathon dance sessions in which they played the female role.

Unbridled power, unfettered influence, a self-absorbed elite. This was Ernest Troubridge's world at the beginning of the twentieth century. The old certainties were being challenged, the old band of brothers being disrupted but the power and the glory of admiralship still obtained. This was the domain of the Silver King.

# 8

## *The Admiralty and Flag Rank, 1908–1914*

Ernest and Una settled down to life at Chatham naval barracks in the commandant's house. Una did not find it altogether congenial, as Ernest 'monopolised her time',[1] expecting her to be home when he returned from his daily duties and to dance attendance on him in his leisure time. She also found Chatham less than exciting or attractive. The entertainment available was not likely to appeal to her; for example, on St Patrick's day 1909 they were both invited to the Warrant Officers' mess for a display of Irish dancing followed by food and drink until 2 am. Ernest insisted that she accompany him.

Troubridge's naval career progressed smoothly and an inspection of his new command in June 1909 showed that his star was still ascendant; the inspector's report noted 'in all respects a well organised establishment which reflects great credit'. But family affairs were less well arranged for in mid-year Una suffered a near fatal ectopic pregnancy which brought with it the long-term consequences of recurrent bouts of salpingitis (salpingitis is an infection and inflammation in the fallopian tubes; its symptoms include pain during ovulation, periods and sexual intercourse).

In September Ernest received a further tribute to his growing reputation when he was appointed Naval Aide-de-Camp to the King, a largely ceremonial post which ran concurrently with his existing posting but nonetheless brought prestige and further exposure to royalty and influence. Initially unpaid, the position was made paid in April 1910 and on the death of Edward in May Ernest was reappointed to serve George V in the same capacity. He was also summoned by Fisher (now First and Principal ADC to the

55

King) to play his part in the funeral of the Fisher's dearly loved King Edward VII, who had died on 6 May. His instructions specified that he was to walk in the procession from Buckingham Palace to Westminster Hall in advance of the body of His Late Majesty 'full uniform to be worn' (Edward would have agreed with that).

Una meanwhile had made a recovery and was once again turning naval heads. Fisher (who had something of a reputation where young ladies were concerned) wrote to Ernest in March 1910 that 'I had the pleasure of meeting Mrs Troubridge at the Abbey and lost my heart ... I hope she got the letter I sent.'[2]

Troubridge's rise and exposure to power was again furthered when he was appointed Private Naval Secretary to the First Lord of the Admiralty, Reginald McKenna, in 1910. McKenna – Cambridge mathematics prize winner, rowing blue, winner of the Grand and Stewards cup at Henley, bridge player and barrister – was an urbane, hands-off and considered politician, and this was an appointment within the First Lord's gift; clearly McKenna had set his heart on Ernest. As early as January he had written to him that he would be pleased 'if you would consent to act as my private secretary'.[3]

The navy was run by the Board of Admiralty. The board consisted of four or five senior officers, usually of flag rank or senior captains, called the Sea Lords. The First Sea Lord was the man in overall command and the person who took the strategic decisions. At the time of Ernest's appointment it was Admiral Sir Arthur Wilson. The First Sea Lord was responsible to the First Lord of the Admiralty, a political appointment of cabinet rank, for the readiness of the fleet and for naval strategy. The First Lord's PNS thus had considerable influence, well above his rank, for he advised the First Lord on many naval matters, both on and off the record and independent of the Sea Lords, and had a key role in advising which officers should be appointed where and who should be promoted.

Una was initially delighted, for it meant that they moved to London, renting a house at 107 St George's Square and allowing her to rejoin the London art set. But it also saw Ernest's three children from his previous marriage, a boy and two girls aged 14, 15 and 16 come to live with them – and they resented the young (23) usurper in the familial nest. It was a challenge that Una would really never master.

Nonetheless, she tried. In 1910 she produced a lovely statuette of Troubridge which excited critical acclaim and on 5 November she gave birth to their first child, Andrea Theodosia, known as 'the Cub' or 'Cubbie'. Quite how Ernest felt at the addition of yet another member to his fractious household is unrecorded, but he no doubt saw it as a tribute to his virility at least.

1911 brought professional pleasure for Troubridge. In March his long-desired promotion to Flag Rank was confirmed and he was made a Rear Admiral. His salary remained as it was but his 'table money' was increased. British admirals were expected to entertain in style! In June both Ernest and Una were invited to the coronation of George V at Westminster Abbey, recognition of their social standing and Ernest's friendship with the king. He was also appointed a Companion of the Bath (CB) – more formally 'additional member of the Third Class, or Companion, of the Most Honourable order of the Bath' as part of the coronation honours.

But in October came an event which would have long-term implications for Troubridge. McKenna, urbane and polished, a financial man who left operational matters to the sailors, was replaced as First Lord by Winston Spencer Churchill, a 37-year-old politician, widely disliked in the naval hierarchy and seen by many as a self-promoting 'mountebank'.

Troubridge remained as his PNS and around this time found himself falling out with Rear Admiral David Beatty over Beatty's desire for specific postings and refusal to accept those offered. With a nice turn of phrase Ernest wrote to Beatty, 'I have your letter today and am truly sorry you have decided to refuse, for one can never tell from day to day whether an appointment afloat will turn out strenuous or otherwise. The fact is that the Admiralty view is that officers should serve where they, i.e. the Admiralty, wish and not where they themselves wish. This is the cold and brutal explanation of your being offered the appointment although I informed the Powers That Be that you did not wish to be offered it.'[4]

Family life was proving more taxing. Una thought that the Troubridge family, children and the extended clan hated her. She confided to her diary that she dreaded the family Christmases, 'eighteen to a table, criticising [her]'.[5]

## Chief of War Staff

As a result of the reforms to the army, driven through by the Secretary of War Haldane between 1906 and 1912, and resultant from the poor performance and preparedness of the British army in the South African Wars at the start of the century, an Army War Staff had been formed to formulate strategy in the event of war and to act as the army's 'brain' – The Imperial General Staff, founded in 1909. Following the Agadir crisis of 1911 when war with Germany began to be a considered possibility it was demonstrated to the satisfaction of the Committee for Imperial Defence (CID, the cabinet committee responsible for Britain's war strategy), and particularly clearly to Haldane and Prime Minister Asquith, that the navy had no coherent war plans and that cooperation and planning between army and navy was non-existent. The politicians insisted that the navy form a war staff, similar to that of the army. The navy, in the person of then First Sea Lord Sir Arthur Wilson, resisted and McKenna supported Wilson.

In this, Wilson was following long naval tradition. Admirals kept their plans in their heads. They did not consult and they did not have a staff. The reason they were admirals was that they knew best and they would decide and dispose alone. Admirals afloat were their own staff, strategist and executor. And in the absence of an admiral, the senior captain present would magically acquire these powers of divination. Fisher had strongly resisted the formation of a staff. He wrote that 'it was a very good organisation for collecting press clippings'.

As a result of Wilson and McKenna's resistance to the idea of a staff both lost their posts, and in October 1911 Churchill became First Lord with the brief of establishing a Naval War Staff, in the teeth of Admiralty opposition. On 8 January 1912 Rear Admiral Ernest Troubridge was appointed to establish and lead it.

Churchill's choice of Troubridge was a puzzle, as there were many officers of higher intellect and greater experience who might have been selected. Beatty, who became Churchill's private naval secretary in succession to Ernest, was one. But Churchill's experience of Troubridge as his naval secretary might have demonstrated to him that Ernest was more tractable than Beatty – and tractability was a quality Churchill prized.

Working for Churchill was a challenging experience. He was hands-on, convinced of his own superiority in all aspects of naval thought, and had taken the retired Fisher as his *eminence grise*. But Troubridge, despite these handicaps, brought the staff into being and tried to execute the mandate he had been given and draw up the navy's war plans. Churchill's new First Sea Lord was Sir Francis Bridgeman, who thought that he and not Churchill should be the man in day-to-day charge. As a result he and his First Lord were soon at loggerheads and Churchill wanted him out. This put Troubridge in a tricky situation as he reported officially to Bridgeman, whom he did not overly respect and who had not been consulted about his appointment. Perhaps with an eye to the main chance, Ernest bypassed Bridgeman at every opportunity, reporting direct to Churchill and giving rise to repeated annoyance from Bridgeman. Churchill eventually got his way, replacing the First Sea Lord with the much more malleable Battenberg by the year's end.

And Ernest's attempts to curry favour did him little good, for he and Churchill soon fell out. Increasingly concerned regarding the German naval threat in the North Sea and around the coasts of the UK, Churchill – driven on by Fisher who now saw the North Sea as the site for a new Trafalgar – wanted to pull most of the British navy out of the Mediterranean and establish a massive superiority in the

North Sea. In particular he wanted to withdraw the battleships from Malta. In 1912 Fisher wrote of his perception that Britain had to strengthen the North Sea at the expense of the Mediterranean, 'As to the policy of reducing the Mediterranean Fleet, the matter is most simple. The margin of power in the North Sea is irreducible and requires this addition of the Mediterranean battleships ... We cannot have everything or be strong everywhere. It is futile to be strong in the subsidiary theatre of war and not overwhelmingly supreme in the decisive theatre. The moral effect of an omnipresent fleet is very great, but it cannot be weighed – at least in the Cabinets of the Powers – against a main fleet known to be ready to strike and able to strike hard.'[6] Many naval officers opposed such plans, as did commercial interests who accused him of leaving the trade routes to British colonies in the Far East unprotected. Churchill reasoned that Britain could reach an agreement with France, whereby the French navy would take over guard duties in the Mediterranean in exchange for a British promise to protect France's northern coast from the German fleet in the event of war. And there was no doubt, Churchill assured the cabinet on 6 May 1912, that the main naval confrontation of the next war would take place in the North Sea – not the Mediterranean. Troubridge had initially opposed this view, arguing that a battle fleet was the only way in which British interests and trade in the Med could be protected and this led to friction as Fisher egged Churchill on and cabinet (especially McKenna who had resented Churchill taking his job) questioned the wisdom of the plans.

Fisher also espoused the theory of 'flotilla defence', whereby large numbers of light (and cheap) craft would be deployed in the North Sea with the battle fleet held to the north to intervene when the enemy was 'fixed', and Churchill adopted the concept, in part for its economy and his need to stabilise the naval estimates. With this in mind, on 1 February 1912 he asked Troubridge to examine the Mediterranean position with a view to leaving only light craft there (also advocated by Fisher). Ernest demurred (see above). But he did continue to work on a plan for the North Sea deployment, as requested, that would adopt the idea of 'intermediate blockade' by light forces. This plan was ready to issue to the CinC Home Fleet by May but a last-minute intervention by Churchill, demanding that it be tested in manoeuvres, both stopped its issuance and infuriated Troubridge. He railed to Bridgeman that his committee's plan was being questioned and set aside by a civilian whose knowledge was not even that of a lieutenant. But it was Ernest's experience and manner that might have been the real problem here. The War Plans Committee which he headed lacked executive authority and he personally was not admired for his intellect, had not held a seagoing command for at least four years and had not commanded as much as a destroyer or cruiser squadron. His opinions did not command respect from senior officers afloat, especially Callaghan, commanding the Home Fleet, who had put a bee in Churchill's ear.

When tested in the summer, the fleet manoeuvres showed the scheme to be seriously flawed. Troubridge's war plan proposed a cordon of 300 miles from Norway to the Dutch coast – an intermediate blockade, as opposed to the close blockade planned for in 1911 and for many years beforehand. This was shown to be unworkable, for the navy did not have enough cruisers or destroyers to support it. Churchill was forced to make an embarrassing climbdown in front of the Committee for Imperial Defence (CID). Troubridge had opposed Churchill regarding the plans for the Med and had put together a strategy for the North Sea, as initially requested, which had gone badly wrong. Churchill, never one to take the blame if it could be pinned on someone else, blamed Troubridge, saying that the cordon system was completely exposed and broken down – as was Ernest's reputation.

Churchill immediately began intriguing against Troubridge. On 12 August he wrote to Prime Minister Asquith requesting that he be allowed to appoint Sir Charles Ottley as Chief of the Naval War Staff. Ottley, a rear admiral on the retired list, had been secretary to the Committee of Imperial Defence for five years, where he was considered to have done an excellent job, and had retired in

February 1912 to take up a lucrative position in civilian life with Armstrong Whitworth & Co. He had, in fact, been Churchill's favoured choice for the post when he first became First Sea Lord. Ottley's terms were high (£2500 a year, plus a house, and a pension of £1000 a year on termination of his employment) but Churchill insisted he was worth it and wrote 'it is not right that we should be denied his services'.[7] In this we may see the invisible hand of Jackie Fisher, for Ottley had been a member of the 'Fishpond' and it was largely as a result of Fisher's urging that he was appointed to the CID in the first place. Nonetheless, the letter shows that Churchill had already decided to get rid of the man who had been his Naval Secretary, and subsequently appointed as his Chief of the Naval War Staff, after less than eight months in post. A scapegoat for Churchill's own failures? A personality clash? Or was Ernest not up to the demands of working for the opinionated and mercurial First Lord? This was certainly Churchill's stated opinion for, in the same letter to Asquith, he intimated that although the war staff had started bravely it required more brain and organising power at the top and that the recent manoeuvres had shown many deficiencies in staff work. He obviously thought Ernest was not up to the job.

So Troubridge was eased out, having held the post for exactly 12 months, and was replaced by Vice-Admiral Sir Henry Jackson, a future First Sea Lord. Churchill wrote to him, 'Your position in the [navy] list makes it impossible for me to offer you the position of 2nd in command in the Mediterranean; but I am vy [sic] glad to be able to offer you the command of the Mediterranean cruisers. The *Defence* is returning from China to exchange with the *Hampshire* and will be available for your Flag-ship.'[8]

Thus Troubridge returned to his beloved Malta and on 6 January 1913 took command of the 1st Cruiser Squadron. Life on Malta was as pleasant as it had been during Ernest's last sojourn. He had his own private box at the Opera House, which he would lend out to his staff when he did not require it. There were amateur dramatics, cricket (*Defence* possessed one of the strongest teams on the island), hockey and football on the Corradino, golf, tennis, and polo on the

Marsa, water polo in the Grand Harbour, bathing at Tyne Bay. The 'fishing fleet' of marriageable ladies migrated to the island every autumn and returned to England in the spring, and provided colourful and charming company for the unwed (and wed!) officer. But not all was sweetness and light.

For meanwhile his family life had continued to be problematic. In November 1912 he had to ask his sisters to take in his 18-year-old daughter Mary as she and Una were not getting on – they were 'like oil and vinegar'[9] and constantly arguing; but this arrangement failed and he eventually took a separate house in Duke Place where all three of his older children would live under the supervision of his spinster sisters.

Una was by now suffering from nausea and sickness, most probably psychosomatic, and she sought help from a hypnotist and psychologist in England. Ernest travelled out to the Med without her while she remained in England for further treatment. Ernest wrote from Malta expressing his unhappiness at her absence but she was in no hurry to set off, preferring the company of her hypnotherapist. Finally, in March 1914, she went out. Troubridge met her in his admiral's barge, lunched her on board the Admiralty yacht *Enchantress* and showed her off on his arm like a prize decoration.

On Malta, because the CinC was unmarried, Una became the 'First Wife'. This entailed an endless round of entertaining as she was expected to make social calls on the other wives and receive them in return. She hated it. She did, however, find the time to start to sing and act with the local opera company. The *Daily Malta Chronicle* commented on her 'cultured voice of remarkable range and sweetness'. And she finished a marble sculpture of the Russian ballet dancer Nijinsky, who had made such an impact in Paris the previous year with his performance in Stravinsky's 'Rite of Spring', occasioning a near riot in the audience. It remains the only such statue of him.

Ernest wanted her to focus on home, child and him, and regarded her sculpture and singing as distractions from these tasks. He had a very traditional view of a wife's role. But she was from a different generation and had real talent and imagination. Intellectually she was his superior and this undermined his self-image. She refused to be deferential to his status or malleable in her personality. And his family disliked her.

By now she had come to abhor the life of the wife of a naval officer and the stultifying round of social duties that it entailed. Whenever possible she sang with the opera company and avoided the navy events. While she sang, Troubridge played golf and tennis all day and went to the races. They were sharing less and less now and Ernest sometimes slept on board his flag-ship rather than with Una ashore. She felt that Troubridge treated her like a possession to show off and was not attentive to her needs. The marriage of the Silver King and Queen was on the rocks.

Successive crises in the Balkans called Troubridge away from Malta, and in the spring and early summer of 1914 he took *Defence* to the coast of Albania as part of an International force protecting citizens and interests while King Wilhelm zu Wied was attempting to preserve his throne and very brief (March to September) reign (see Appendix 5). German representation was provided by the light cruiser SMS *Breslau*, a ship which will feature again in this story as Troubridge's enemy and opponent. For now they were allies and British officers were entertained on the German ship (and noticed its deck cargo of mines, not a usual cargo in peacetime).

With the assassination of the Austrian Archduke, and as the world lurched towards war, Ernest exercised his guns and left the King to his fate. On 30 July *Defence* sailed back to Malta on a war footing, pausing only to bury at sea a sailor who had died of enteric fever.

## The Rear Admiral, 1914

Troubridge had risen without trace. Without appearing to be involved in any particular success during his forty years in the service, attaching his name to any public achievement or being seen as an intellect of any note, he was now the second most powerful British sailor in the Med. He had pedigree and lineage but had fought in no great battle or even minor skirmish to prove it. In this he was different from many of his peers in this narrative. Rear Admiral Cradock, commanding the 4th Cruiser Squadron on the North American station, had fought in Egypt and the Sudan and distinguished himself in the Boxer rebellion of 1900. David Beatty, who had succeeded him as PNS to Churchill, and now commanded the battle cruisers of the Grand Fleet, had fought at Omdurman and in the Boxer conflict; Jellicoe, CinC of the Grand Fleet, had been severely wounded in China; Meux, at Portsmouth, had fought with the naval brigade at Ladysmith. Pakenham, now commanding the 3rd Light Cruiser Squadron, had sat in a deckchair on the gun deck of the Japanese flag-ship during the Battle of Tsushima in his white tropical uniform. When a shell exploded nearby, killing sailors and covering his uniform with blood, he calmly went to his cabin, changed into a new rig and resumed his place in the deckchair. Arthur Wilson had won a Victoria Cross at the Battle of El Teb.

But Troubridge had not been tested in battle and his courage under fire was unproven, although accepted; after all had he not bravely rescued the sailor at Suda Bay? He was 'a magnificent figure of a man, a born leader, although he had not a creative brain or much interest in weapons development'.[10] Neither was he considered bright. Major Adrian Grant-Duff of the Imperial Defence Secretariat, who had worked with Ernest while the latter was COS, said of him, 'Ballard [Director Operations Division at the Admiralty] has more brains in his little finger that Troubridge has in his great woolly head.'[11] Ernest's ancestry, his bluff, open demeanour and reputation for honest speaking, his imposing rugged countenance and genial lines around the eyes, his instantly recognisable hair, his friendship with royalty, his younger and attractive artist wife – all conveyed a reassuring air of solidity, of competence, of trustworthiness. This was the man who went to war.

# 9

## Opening Shots, 27 July to 6 August 1914

Troubridge's superior officer in the Mediterranean and the CinC of the Mediterranean Fleet was Admiral Sir Archibald Berkeley Milne, himself also the son of an admiral and baronet who became First Naval Lord under both Gladstone and Disraeli, and grandson of another admiral. In 1884 Ernest had briefly served under him in the royal yacht *Victoria and Albert*. In appearance Milne was affected, sporting a non-regulation stiff turned-down collar and bow tie, a white, trimmed beard and luxuriant black moustache. He was a snob of the worst kind. Once his sleeve was brushed by a passing seaman – Milne took out his handkerchief, flicked some imagined dirt from his sleeve with it and threw the contaminated linen over the side. He was also one of those admirals who owed their position to Royal influence rather than ability.

After service in the Zulu war as an ADC to Lord Chelmsford, and escaping the massacre at Isandlwana, Milne rose to the rank of captain in the navy before accepting the post of captain of HM Yacht *Osborne*, a post usually held by a commander, reasoning that exposure to royalty offered him better hopes of promotion. Such posts were often seen as mixed blessings for they lacked any martial qualities, but Milne loved the ceremony and obsessive spit and polish of service in the Royal Squadron and went on to command the royal yachts from 1903 to 1905. He became good friends with King Edward VII and, especially, Queen Alexandra who nicknamed him 'Arky-Barky', an appellation which soon got round the fleet to humorous effect. A fellow officer asserted that Milne's hobbies were collecting rare orchids and entertaining royal ladies. Never an intellect (he is recorded as saying, 'They don't pay me to think, they pay me to be an admiral'[1]) and lacking any combat experience he was nonetheless promoted through royal influence to flag rank, and in 1912 Winston Churchill, First Lord of the Admiralty and under pressure from George V, made him Admiral commanding the Mediterranean fleet.

Jackie Fisher loathed Milne and was appalled (he called him Sir Berkley Mean, 'He buys his newspapers second hand,') not just because of his royal connections but also because he was a leading Beresfordite and had intended to testify against Fisher at the CID sub-committee of 1909, until he saw which way the wind was blowing and backed out. Fisher wrote to Churchill, 'You are aware that Sir Berkeley Milne is unfitted to be the senior Admiral afloat, as you have made him … I can't believe that you foresee all the consequences. The results would be Irreparable, Irremediable, Eternal!'[2] He also vowed to cut off any communication with Churchill (a vow he did not keep). In further letters he identified Churchill's fear of his wife's ostracism at Court as the reason that had led him to make the appointment, and said a 'wicked wrong' had been done. Among the correspondents he shared these views with was Ernest; in a letter of April 1912 he expressed his shock at the appointment. And to Lord Esher he wrote 'Winston has sacrificed the country to the court.'[3]

Milne's appointment was for a period of three years but as the storm clouds of war billowed, change was mooted. In order to maximise the navy's presence in the North Sea and Channel, Britain agreed with France that France would take the lead in the Med, concentrating its navy there and thus allowing Britain to reinforce the home waters. The French would therefore command in the Med in time of war and the French Fleet commander would be the senior officer afloat. In 1914 this was Vice-Admiral Boué Lapeyrere. As he was junior in rank to Milne this would cause complications of formality and protocol, and it was planned instead to appoint Milne to the CinC Nore command and leave Troubridge to command British forces in the Mediterranean by himself. This change was

Admiral Berkeley Milne

designated to take place on 30 August – the outbreak of war intervened, however. Thus Milne, botanist and unmarried collector of Titled Ladies, found himself in command of a shooting war.

The British Fleet under his command was smaller than in the days of Malta's past glories but still a substantial force, comprising three of Fisher's 'greyhounds of the sea', 12-inch gunned battle cruisers, four armoured cruisers, four light cruisers and sixteen destroyers. Opposed to it were three potential enemies (the *soi disant* 'triple alliance'). The German Mittelmeer-Division of two ships, SMS *Goeben* and *Breslau*, a battle cruiser with 11-inch guns and a light cruiser; the Austrian navy; and the Italian navy. Of these it was thought that the Italians might well renege on their treaty agreement and remain neutral, but the Austrians would be an enemy and although of limited utility they possessed the advantage of the threat of the 'fleet in being'. And the German ships were top notch vessels presenting a significant threat.

The Kaiser's two ships were commanded by Vice-Admiral Wilhelm Souchon. Short in height, with a stubby beard, close-cropped hair and untidy in his dress, he was the antithesis of the dandyish Milne. He was regarded as an aggressive and capable officer who combined a Germanic thoroughness with a rather more Gallic charm and geniality, perhaps as a result of his family's Huguenot roots. He was to prove a more than resourceful enemy.

## Milne's initial orders

In the event of war, the French battle plans called for the swift reinforcement of their European-based armies by the transhipment from French African possessions of the troops based there, via Algerian ports to Toulon. Thus Milne's original orders, dated 30 July, and originally drafted in Churchill's hand: 'Your first task should be to aid the French in transportation of their African Army by covering and, if possible, bringing to action fast individual German ships, particularly *Goeben*, who may interfere with that transportation

... do not at this stage be brought to action against superior forces except in combination with the French as part of a general battle ... the speed of your squadron should enable you to choose your moment.'[4] In these orders was the germ of future problems, for they contained more than enough ambiguity and inexact drafting. 'Superior force' was not defined; Milne's attention was focused firmly on the French transit; the need to neutralise the *Goeben* was not stressed. Milne was not a man to deal with ambiguity well or use his initiative. It is also important to note that at this time Britain and Germany were not at war (and would not be until the expiry of the British ultimatum at midnight on 4 August). Neither were France and Germany formally at war until 3 August. And nobody knew whether the Austrians would sortie – although many believed that Souchon would head for the Adriatic to join forces with them before they took any action.

Milne replied on the 31st to the effect that he had too few ships with which to implement these orders, and would therefore concentrate in order to assist the French fleet with his cruisers and light cruisers dispersed to protect trade routes and would ignore the eastern Mediterranean. The Admiralty then instructed him on 2 August that *Goeben* must be shadowed by his battle cruisers and the approach to the Adriatic watched by cruisers; he was further instructed to personally remain near Malta.

Now Milne ordered Troubridge to sail from Malta to the mouth of the Adriatic with three of his four big cruisers (the fourth, *Black Prince*, joined on 4 August having been abortively despatched to Marseille and then re-called) and eight destroyers but also with *Indomitable* and *Indefatigable*, two battle cruisers, in company. However these latter two ships were detached on 3 August to watch for the *Goeben* west of Sicily, as a result of Admiralty orders. Demonstrating an unwillingness to use his brain or initiative at all, Troubridge cabled back to Milne that he wished to be ordered as to whether ships watching the Adriatic should continue to watch the entrance or carry out the orders of 30 July – by which he meant shadow or tackle the *Goeben* – should the *Goeben* sortie (at this point war had not been declared). Acting in line with his orders from the Admiralty, Milne replied that a watch should still be kept but that *Goeben* was the primary consideration and the Admiralty soon confirmed this to CinC: 'Watch in mouth of Adriatic should be maintained but *Goeben* is your objective.'[5]

Meanwhile, *Goeben* and her consort arrived at Messina, Sicily, also on 2 August to coal and departed thence to shell the French embarkation ports of Bone and Philppeville on the morning of 4 August. They caused damage but also confusion as nobody knew where they would go next. Milne certainly believed that they would head for Gibraltar and the Atlantic, as did many in the Admiralty and he was instructed to send battle cruisers to guard the Straits of Gibraltar to prevent the enemy's exit; instead, during the course of the day of 4 August, Souchon headed back to Messina, shadowed by two British battle cruisers and the cruiser *Dublin*. Germany and England were not yet at war – had a shooting match started the odds were in favour of the British but the rules of war had to be obeyed. The same day, Milne signalled that *Indomitable* and *Indefatigable* were shadowing the enemy (initially at 22 knots!) to which Churchill responded 'very good, hold her, war imminent'. Through heroic efforts in the engine room, Souchon was able to pull away from his pursuers and by 2100 hours he was out of sight. (The battle cruisers first sighted *Goeben* at 0945 on 4 August and trailed her from that time until they lost sight of her at 2100. Milne and his command had taken in an Admiralty signal at 1900 that the British ultimatum to Germany expired at midnight GMT).

Milne now suspected that Souchon was back at Messina, as he subsequently proved to be; and he then threw away the perfect chance to bottle him up and destroy him. Troubridge with his four armoured cruisers was at the southern end of the Messina strait watching the Adriatic for a break out by the Austrian fleet. The light cruiser *Chatham* was at the northerly exit, guarding that entrance. If Milne had sent his two battle cruisers to reinforce *Chatham* and his third to Troubridge, the *Goeben* would have been forced to fight her way out and would most likely have been sunk or badly damaged.

But Milne was still fixated on the orders of 30 July and his attention was to the west. Influenced by another Admiralty telegram of 4 August which told him that Italy should not be antagonised and that her territorial six mile limit should be respected (which, by the way, meant that technically he could not enter the Messina straits), and by the instruction of the same date to send battle cruisers to watch the Straits of Gibraltar, he sent one battle cruiser to coal and took the other two to patrol between Sicily and Tunisia, thus positioned for a break out to the west by *Goeben* in an attempt to interfere with the French shipping and escape to the Atlantic Ocean. To Troubridge he repeated an Admiralty order that he is 'not to get engaged seriously with superior forces'.[6]

On 6 August the Admiralty signalled Milne that if *Goeben* went south through the Straits of Messina he could follow her, irrespective of previous orders to the contrary; but Milne's dispositions meant that he was in no position to do so and so the German squadron left Messina, well clear of any British ship except the *Gloucester*, Souchon feinted towards the Adriatic but then steered to the south-east for Cape Matapan. *Gloucester* hung on to her and signalled that the enemy were heading to the south. Now only Troubridge and his squadron stood between the Germans and their escape to the east. The Silver King's chance had come.

*Goeben*'s move came as Troubridge was patrolling off Cephalonia, a good place to be had Souchon made for the Austrian port of Pola. He immediately steamed north with the intention of engaging the Germans near Corfu – thinking the turn to the south-east a feint, he did not himself turn to the south until just after midnight at the junction of the 6/7 August. The defining moment of his career had come.

# 10

## The Opposing Forces

Before examining Troubridge's actions on 6 and 7 August in more detail, it is relevant to consider the relative strengths of the forces ranged against each other in the seas around Cephalonia.

Ernest's key striking force comprised his four armoured cruisers, HMS *Defence*, *Duke of Edinburgh*, *Black Prince*, and *Warrior*. They formed a largely heterogeneous force, despite representing three different classes of warship.

The armoured cruiser was a class of warship developed in the late nineteenth century, designed like other types of cruisers to operate as a long-range, independent unit, capable of defeating any ship apart from a battleship and fast enough to outrun any battleships it encountered. It was distinguished from other types of cruiser by its belt armour of iron (or later steel) plating on much of the hull to protect the ship from shellfire, much like the protection method of battleships, and differed from the latter class by its designed long range, speed and coal carrying capability. The size of armoured cruisers varied; the largest were as large and expensive as battleships, and often required a larger or similar size of crew owing to their need for more boilers (to give both speed and range) than a battleship (and at full speed they generally needed more stokers). As a type they were made obsolete by the development of the battle cruiser, fast, heavily armed capital ships, and the increasing speeds of battleships them-selves as turbine and (eventually) oil technology became prevalent. Ernest's quartet represented the last flowering of the breed as they were launched the same year, or later, as Jackie Fisher's revolutionary *Dreadnought* and his first battle cruisers of the *Invincible* class.

The 1904 edition of the *Encyclopaedia Americana* (written well before the launch of Ernest's ships) quotes a Captain Walker, of the United States navy, describing the role of the armoured cruiser as 'that of a vessel possessing in a high degree offensive and defensive qualities, with the capacity of delivering her attack at points far distant from her base in the least space of time'. The same entry defined an armoured cruiser as 'a battleship in which the qualities of offense and defense have been much reduced to gain high speed and great coal capacity,' and adds, '... there are many who hold that the armoured cruiser is an anomaly, something less than a battleship and more than a protected cruiser, performing satisfactorily the duties of neither, with no special function of her own and lacking the great desideratum in warships, ability to fight in proportion to her great size and cost'.

HMS *Defence*

*Defence*, the flag-ship of the 1st Cruiser Squadron, was a Minotaur class vessel, mounting four 9.2-inch guns in two double turrets; ten 7.5-inch and sixteen 12-pounder quickfirers together with five torpedo tubes completed her offensive capabilities. She was completed in 1909, by which time she had already been made obsolete, displaced 14,600 tons and had a design speed of 23 knots. Reflecting the beliefs of the time in which she was designed, her armour belt was thickest amidships at 6 inches, tapering to 3 inches at the stem and stern but only 1.5–2 inches on the deck. Ships were expected to engage at close range (Wilson, First Sea Lord in 1911, believed 5,000 yards) and thus would expect to receive largely horizontal fire, not plunging fire (a belief which was later to cost the navy dear at Jutland in 1916).

*Black Prince* and *Duke of Edinburgh* were slightly older ships for the same class (and the first ships designed by Naval Director of Construction Phillip Watts). They sported six 9.2-inch guns backed up by ten 6-inch quickfirers and three torpedo tubes. Their design speed was 23 knots (although *Black Prince* never got beyond 20.5) and they had the same belt armour as *Defence* but even less deck armour, 0.75–1.5 inches.

Finally *Warrior*, dating from 1906, carried an arsenal of six 9.2-inch guns with four 7.5-inch, twenty-six 3-pounders, a design speed of 23 knots, three torpedo tubes and the same deck and side armour as *Black Prince* and *Duke of Edinburgh*.

The mixed armament of heavy guns, typical of the time they were built, made spotting fall of shot (and hence accuracy) difficult and the maximum gunnery range was some 16,000 yards. But together they were a strong force, capable of a combined broadside of 8,480 pounds and, of course, able to manoeuvre separately as four different gun platforms.

In company Troubridge had three light cruisers, not able to take place in a line of battle but a match (and more) for the *Breslau* and eight destroyers, giving him a torpedo attack option.

In contrast to the British armoured cruisers, the *Goeben* was a modern ship, launched in 1911 as part of the German response to the *Dreadnought* revolution. She was a splendid modern battle cruiser with an armament of ten 11-inch guns in five turrets and twelve 6-inch quickfirers, twelve 24-pounders and four torpedo tubes. With a design speed of 28 knots she was the fastest ship in the Mediterranean; and in armour she was the best protected, with an 11-inch belt amidships and 3 inches on deck. Firing broadsides she could bring all ten big guns to bear coupled with six of the 6-inch weapons, giving a weight of shell of 8,272 pounds; her big guns could range up to 24,000 yards. Thus she was capable of outpacing Troubridge's force, outranging them and delivering a similar weight of shot. She was a formidable foe. In company Souchon had the light cruiser *Breslau*, like the British light cruisers not intended for line of battle and additionally less well armed.

Milne's three battle cruisers – each a match for the *Goeben* – were too far away to be of any immediate reckoning.

But all was not quite as it seemed. *Goeben* had ongoing problems with her boiler tubes (and indeed Souchon had replacements shipped out and fitted just before the outbreak of war) and maintaining her top speed for long was difficult. She was alone in the Med with no chance for the resupply of any more engine room equipment. Her ammunition was a finite quantity with no possibility of obtaining any more without breaking out to the Atlantic or Adriatic. She needed ongoing coaling which, as the British tightened their grip on the trade routes, would become problematic. *Goeben* was a strong force; but she was not well placed for long-term success and was heavily outnumbered in quantity of opponents.

Furthermore, Souchon had an ace up his sleeve. German diplomats and government had been negotiating with Turkey for the Turks to enter the war on the side of the Triple Alliance. Unbeknown to the British, Enver Pasha, Naval Minister and pro-German, had given implicit permission for the *Goeben* to enter Turkish waters. This had been passed to Souchon and although later revoked it gave him the escape route he needed. Souchon was not going anywhere near the Atlantic and Milne's capital ships. He was going to force the Dardanelles and enter Turkish waters.

# 11

## HMS *Defence, 5–7 August*

*Defence* had made early preparations for war. On 1 August she had gone into dry dock for cleaning and repainting her foul bottom, and her funnel markings were painted out to confuse enemy spotters. On 2 August she took on ammunition and a coal lighter came alongside to take off all private possessions. At 2140 Troubridge gave the order to proceed to sea, firing a gun and flying the Blue Peter to attract the attention of men dallying on shore. Already, on the voyage from Durazzo to Malta, all store rooms had been re-stocked to give room for stopping up any hits in her sides. She was prepared for a fight.

Ernest received the general signal to commence hostilities on 5 August. Immediately he signalled by flag to his squadron that if the *Goeben* tried to enter the Adriatic he would give battle. However, he expressed concerns over their relative gunnery ranges and thus informed his captains that he might retreat initially to draw the enemy into waters where his guns would be in range. Already he was showing a preoccupation with Souchon's ability to out-shoot his own ships. He later signalled to Milne that he was keeping off the coast of Santa Maura and would, if *Goeben* were sighted, attempt to draw her into narrower waters where her gunnery advantage would be nullified. The ship prepared for battle, throwing all unnecessary items – especial the flammable ones – over the side, including the captain's office desks.

The same day, receiving the word that *Goeben* was at Messina, Ernest detached the *Gloucester* from his squadron to watch the southern entrance. Sure enough at 1815 on 6 August *Gloucester* signalled that *Goeben* had left the port and subsequently that she was steering for the Adriatic (this was Souchon's 'feint').

Troubridge made his dispositions on that basis. He signalled to his squadron that he proposed to arrive at Fano Island at day break and use the shoal waters around the island to try to choose his range (although quite why Souchon should oblige him in this was not addressed), his orders prohibiting him from engaging them in the middle of the strait (he had received no such specific orders in fact, other than to avoid serious battle with a superior force).

But then Captain Howard Kelly on the *Gloucester* signalled Souchon's turn to the south and it became clear that Troubridge was about 140 miles to the north-east of her position; which meant that by sailing due south he could place his ships across *Goeben's* line of advance – the 'crossing the T' so beloved of naval planners. At 0245 on 7 August he signalled his ships that this was exactly his objective and, on encountering the enemy, they should form a line ahead; in other words his ships would all be able to fire broadsides at an enemy coming head on, and thus unable to deploy their full firepower.

In crossing an opponent's T, a fleet commander achieves maximum advantage; it was classic naval doctrine for the time and in planning thus Ernest was exactly following the path he would have been expected to. His signal to his light cruisers of 0254 ('1st Cruiser Squadron position 2.30 a.m. . . . course south. Am endeavouring to cross *Goeben* bows at 6 a.m.'[1]) confirmed his thinking. He also ordered Captain John Kelly (brother of Howard) in *Dublin* with two destroyers to make a night torpedo attack in order to slow *Goeben* down. (*Dublin* had been despatched to Troubridge by Milne on 6 August with two destroyers to reinforce the 1st CS should *Goeben* come south. *Dublin*, however, having arrived at the anticipated point of juncture at 0400, failed to locate the *Goeben*).

And yet by 0347 he had abandoned the chase. What happened to make him change his mind and ignore Nelson's dictum (and no doubt his great grandfather's too) that no captain could do wrong who put his ship alongside the enemy?

What happened, according to Troubridge's later evidence, was

Fawcet Wray. Wray was Captain of HMS *Defence* and Ernest's Flag-Captain – his right-hand man. Arrogant and self-satisfied, a gunnery expert and previously an instructor at the navy's gunnery school (and, as a lieutenant, the inventor of a prototype range clock for fire control), Wray had been with Troubridge since the latter's appointment to command the 1st Cruiser Squadron. Troubridge, who had little interest in – or knowledge of – the technicalities of the gunnery art, left such matters to Wray, who had conducted the regular squadron gunnery inspections.

At about 0245 Wray went to Ernest's position (he was using the chart house; Wray was in the wheel house next door) and asked him if he was going to fight, 'because if so the squadron ought to know'. At 0300 Troubridge signalled Milne that he was going to engage *Goeben* at around 0600. To Wray he sighed, 'I know it is wrong but I cannot let the name of the whole Mediterranean squadron stink.'[2]

Around this time he received the news that the *Dublin* had failed to find the *Goeben* (it later transpired they had probably sailed past each other in the night) and that his destroyers were running out of coal. The problems crowded in. Never an intellectual, Ernest was having difficulty working out what to do. His orders, as he saw them, told him not to engage a superior force. He believed that, given the range and speed issues, *Goeben* was such. His destroyers, which might have made useful torpedo raids, were in need of fuel. And yet he knew that tradition enjoined him to attack.

At 0330 Wray again entered Ernest's cabin. 'I do not like it sir,' was his opening gambit. 'Neither do I; but why?' Ernest replied. Wray then went on to describe his conception of how the battle would unfold. The battle cruisers were still heading back to Malta so there was no hope of heavy support. Given the good visibility, *Goeben* would sight the 1st Cruiser Squadron out of range of the squadron's guns. She could then circle round at a radius of over 16,000 yards and pick off the ships one by one. It would, said Wray, 'be the suicide of the squadron'. Ernest enquired if it would be possible to close to a range at which his guns would bear. 'No sir', responded Wray, 'but I will send for the navigator.'

'I cannot turn away now, think of my pride,' Ernest mused. 'Has your pride got anything to do with this sir?' replied Wray. 'It is the country's welfare which is at stake.'[3] Wray then returned to the bridge and left Ernest and the navigator closeted.

It is not easy at this distance to imagine the turmoil in Troubridge's mind. Already wavering about his decision to engage in open seas, Wray, his expert in matters ballistic, had confirmed to him that he could not hope to successfully take on his opponent. He would be condemning his ships and his men – and himself – to death if he continued with his action.

After some moments the navigator returned to the bridge. 'The Admiral wants us to alter course to south 30 east,'[4] he informed Wray. At 0347 *Defence* turned slightly towards land and slowed. The 1st Cruiser Squadron, pride of the Mediterranean, commanded by the descendant of Nelson's band of brothers, had turned away from the enemy. Not only had he turned away, he had given up the chase. The *Goeben* was free to go where she pleased. Actually not quite free – for the stubborn, imposingly tall, sardonic Howard Kelly in *Gloucester* still hung on to the fleeing enemy, despite twice being ordered by Milne to give up the chase for fear of being captured or sunk and once having to evade a salvo from the German battle cruiser. Kelly finally gave up the chase at 1712 on 7 August having pursued a vastly superior enemy for 23 hours and in doing so setting an example which put Troubridge's decision not to continue his pursuit in a rather tawdry light.

Wray, meanwhile, following the change of course, had revisited Troubridge's cabin. 'Admiral that is the bravest thing you have ever done in your life,' he stated. Ernest, he later reported, was in tears.[5]

Wray had not expected Troubridge to call off the pursuit and it troubled him. At 0415 he approached the Admiral again and suggested that they should follow *Gloucester* 'to give her something to fall back on'.[6] But Troubridge declined. He had by now informed Milne and asked him for instructions ('Being only able to meet *Goeben* outside the range of my guns I have abandoned the chase with my squadron; request instructions'). The buck was passed. It was no longer his problem. Milne's response, 'Why did you not continue to chase *Goeben*, she only [*sic*] going 17 knots and important to bring her to action,'[7] only caused him, for the first of many times, to rehearse his defence. 'I would consider it a great imprudence to place squadron in such a position as to be picked off at leisure and sunk while unable to effectively reply. The decision is not the easiest of the two to make I am well aware.'[8]

Milne continued his dilatory way back to Malta, signalling the Admiralty at 0500 that the chase had been abandoned and at 1430 that, after coaling at Malta, his three battle cruisers and a light cruiser would search for *Goeben* again. Additionally, and showing his preoccupation with his original orders, he reported that the watch on the Adriatic was being maintained.

Now fate took a leading role. On 8 August, as Milne was making his way back towards Crete and the last sighting of the *Goeben*, an overzealous Admiralty clerk saw an unsent telegram for CinC Med and decided to send it. It commanded Milne to commence operations against Austria. He immediately altered course for the Adriatic and gave up his search for the *Goeben*. But the telegram was in fact in error – it had been prepared to save time when needed. Britain was not at war with Austria. By the time the mistake was corrected (9 August at 1250 – 'Not at war with Austria, continue chase of *Goeben*') any faint hope he might have had of catching the German ships had gone, although Milne continued his stately progress east at no more than 10 knots, leaving Troubridge to again guard the Adriatic (if one German was too much for him, how was he going to cope with the Austrian fleet?)

On 10 August Souchon steamed into the Dardanelles, demanded passage from the signal station, was allowed through and anchored in the harbour of Istanbul; and on the 12th, his two ships were officially 'sold' to the Turkish navy and he became a Turkish admiral and fleet commander. The escape of the *Goeben*, the direct consequence of Troubridge's action in the morning of 7 August, had brought Turkey into the war on the German side.

Milne, on hearing the news, predictably placed the blame on the Admiralty for not telling him where Souchon might be headed and on Troubridge for his failure to intercept and engage the *Goeben*.

There are more than a few puzzling facets of Troubridge's decision to turn away. One in particular stands out. The navy was a top-down, command and control organisation. Admirals knew best and they alone took decisions. They were demi-gods afloat and possessed of all wisdom – staffs were there to execute, not help decide. When Cradock, three months later, took the decision to sail from the Falklands and find and fight the opposing German squadron, he took the decision himself; he consulted no one, not even his flag-captain. When Jellicoe, two years later, had to decide how to deploy his fleet at Jutland, he didn't ask for opinions; he stood alone on the bridge, thought the problem through, and then issued the orders – alone; by himself.

Yet, at 0330 in the morning, a senior admiral, lifelong navy man, of heroic lineage, taking his ships towards an engagement which, even if he suffered losses, must bring further glory to him, his family name and his beloved navy, turned away on the basis of a few minutes' conversation with his flag-captain. Why did he allow himself to be swayed by a few words from his subordinate? Wray was within his rights to voice his concerns, but Ernest did not have to listen to them and Wray was relatively junior in his rank having only three years' tenure. Indeed tradition would almost dictate that the admiral ignore his captain. Troubridge later stated that there was a 'mental struggle between my natural desire to fight and my sense of duty in view of my orders'. But this was the most important decision of his life; and in most people's minds he 'bottled it'. Why?

He was 52 years of age and had never commanded in a real fight before. He was not famous for his intellect. Marital troubles hung around him, he had been (unfairly in his mind) moved on from his position at the Admiralty war staff. He was under pressure and the situation was not clear cut.

Or was it that Troubridge was one of the few officers in the navy

82

who had witnessed the devastation that modern shellfire can cause – and the ranges at which this could be brought about – from his time as an observer in the Russo-Japanese conflict of 1904? Did this weigh vividly in his mind? Did he hear in his mind the smash of shell into his charthouse cabin as he took his decision? Did this make him believe that *Goeben* was a superior force? Was it the results of the 1913 manoeuvres when he and his squadron sighted the British battle cruiser HMS *Lion* (one of the 'big cats' with 13-inch guns) on the horizon? Troubridge met her 'almost out of sight' where he 'never dreamt of opening fire'; but 'in a moment half my squadron were adjudged by the Chief Umpire to be out of action to her fire'.[9] Or was he obsessed with his own sense of strategic awareness? During his time as Chief of Staff at the Admiralty he had been criticised for his strategies but had vigorously defended them. Did he believe that strategically he knew best? Finally, was it a resentment of Milne, his superior? Milne, he knew, should not have been in command at all, as he was supposed to be back in England; only the outbreak of war had kept him in post. He, Troubridge, should now have been in command of the Mediterranean fleet; Milne too had taken his battle cruiser support away from him. Was it resentment that drove him; a desire to say, 'If you are in command then you can take the difficult decisions'? A fit of pique perhaps?

In later argument Troubridge simply maintained that he was obeying his orders. During his written report to the Admiralty of 25 August he argued that although his squadron was eager and ready to fight he was placed in a cruel position; he saw the *Goeben* as a superior force and he was ordered not to engage such an enemy. Was that really the reason?

## Witnesses

The future Admiral of the Fleet, Viscount Cunningham of Hynd-hope, was with Troubridge's squadron as Commander of the destroyer *Scorpion*. Cunningham, later to be a famously aggressive and attack-minded admiral during the Second World War, subsequently wrote about the incident. His destroyer, in company with others, was suffering from fuel shortage due to the non-arrival of a collier, but he noted 'it was at daylight that we had another signal to say that Admiral Troubridge had abandoned the chase. I will not comment on that decision.'[10] It is easy to imagine that had Cunningham been in command the orders might have been different, although he did go on to note that 'we all wondered what had happened to the battle-cruisers'.[11]

Another witness was Paymaster Commander (later Rear Admiral) Henry Horniman, who was serving on Milne's flag-ship, HMS *Inflexible*. Among his duties was the coding and deciphering of messages and he was about that duty during the early morning of 7 August. In an unpublished autobiography he describes how Milne came to sit with him at 0300 as they awaited news from the 1st Cruiser Squadron. He and Milne talked about Troubridge and the orders that he had been given 'to steer a course to meet the *Goeben* at dawn. There was only one signal expected,' he wrote. 'The explicit orders Troubridge had been given' was how he expressed his understanding of the situation '[we] had no doubt of them being carried out'.[12]

'At 0400 the expected signal from *Defence* was brought to me,' he continued. 'I immediately decrypted it and my heart was fairly in my boots when I handed it to the Admiral.'[13] Milne took it in a 'noble' fashion and retired to his cabin 'with no sign of "discomposition"'. Horniman noted that 'Troubridge had changed his mind, had altered course and the Germans had passed on.'[14]

Captain Richard Phillimore, Chief of Staff to Milne, was also on board *Inflexible*. In his personal log he noted that 'it was hoped that 1st Cruiser Squadron would bring her [the *Goeben*] to action as she was shaping course for Cape Matapan but RA1CS [Troubridge] reported that "I have abandoned chase with my squadron".' He added that 'it was suddenly discovered that the ten destroyers with the RA1CS had not been kept full up with coal ... this was very startling in view of the fact that all except *Scorpion* had been reported as having 75 tons on board the previous day.[15] Some poor staff work by Troubridge in 1st CS is the implication.

Henry Fitch, Assistant-Paymaster on board *Defence*, noted that 'the disappointment on *Defence* was intense'.[16]

Finally, the comments of Captain George Borrett, commanding HMS *Warrior*, probably serve for the whole squadron. Speaking to Horniman, his friend of many years, he noted that 'the whole squadron was on tiptoe with gratified expectation of an immediate engagement and were horrified at the shameful denouement'.[17]

The British and French Admiralties having finally decided that they were at war with Austria, on 14/15 August Troubridge was ordered to operate with his destroyers and *Defence* only in cooperation with the French fleet against the Austrian fleet in the Adriatic. However, the sweep produced poor reward, sinking only one small Austrian cruiser. When Ernest asked permission of Boué de Lapeyrere, the French force commander, to send his destroyers to rescue the surviving enemy sailors he was refused, with the rather Gallic comment that it was now 'too late'.

Milne returned to the UK and Troubridge was made Senior Naval Officer Dardanelles, having transferred his flag to the battle cruiser HMS *Indefatigable*. On 8 September, at 1745 hours, he received the following signal from Churchill: 'Your duty is to sink the *Goeben* and *Breslau* under whatever flag, if they come out of the Dardanelles.' The sound of a door swinging shut on an empty stable resounded through the fleet.

# 12

## *Outrage, August 1914*

Back home in Britain, the initial public reaction to the *Goeben*'s escape was not negative. It was viewed as a 'sweeping the seas' operation, the Germans driven out of the Med. Milne's lack of initiative, the Admiralty's lack of clarity, and Troubridge's failure to engage were ignored by the popular press. Indeed, the Admiralty itself expressed satisfaction with Milne's behaviour and dispositions in a press release of 30 August ('They prevented the Germans from carrying out their primary role of preventing French troops crossing from Africa ... The conduct and dispositions of Admiral Sir Berkeley Milne in regard to the German vessels *Goeben* and *Breslau* have been the subject of the careful examination of the Board of Admiralty, with the result that their Lordships have approved the measures taken by him in all respects'). Milne returned to the UK on 18 August fully expecting to take up his promised appointment of the Nore command.

Later it slowly dawned on the press that Turkey would become an enemy (eventually on 30 October) and with two new ships to confront Russia and the Allies in the Black Sea; and that the failure of Troubridge to engage the German ships had barred the Black Sea as a route to reinforce Russia and damaged British prestige (and would eventually lead to the disastrous Dardanelles campaign). Not only could the *Goeben* help the Ottomans against the Greeks, it could also help them against the Russians who, according to *The Times* in an article dated 9 September, 'had no vessels in the Black Sea comparable to the *Goeben* as regards age and power, and her battleships in commission, though powerful enough, are handicapped by

86

the speed of the German battle cruiser, which could literally steam round any one of them.'

In those parts of the Admiralty that mattered there was fury. Battenberg, First Sea Lord, minuted, 'Not one of the excuses which Ad Troubridge gives can be accepted for one moment. The escape of the *Goeben* must remain a shameful episode in the war. The flag officer responsible for this failure cannot be entrusted with any further command afloat and his continuance in such command constitutes a danger to the State.'[1] Fisher, fulminating from the sidelines, wrote, 'Personally I should have shot Sir Berkley Milne for the *Goeben*, like Byng.' Milne 'had no excuse for not surrounding Messina with his whole force ... close up ... as if International Law mattered a damm ... and the Italians would have loved him for it,'[2] He pleaded with Churchill's private secretary, 'Surely he is not going to be given the Nore after such utterly effete incapacity.' From there on Fisher always referred to him as 'Sir Berkley Goeben'. As for Troubridge, whom Fisher had previously assiduously courted, he raged, 'Any dammed fool can obey orders.' (In this statement Fisher would have been supported by the army and its Field Regulations of 1914 in which [Part 1, Ch. II, para 13] does not merely encourage a subordinate to disobey the orders of a commander not present it effectively requires him to: 'If a subordinate, in the absence of a superior, neglects to depart from the letter of his orders when such a departure is clearly demanded by circumstances, and failure ensues, he will be held responsible for such failure.')

But Milne prepared a very thorough defence of his actions, basing it on the orders that he had regularly received from the Admiralty; he stated clearly that he considered his first priority to protect the French transports, as so ordered. In a fifty-page report he identified the six clear objectives that the Admiralty had telegraphed to him and how he had complied with them. He was prepared for a fight in a way he seemed not to be when actually in command at sea.

And although initially refused an interview on his return to England, Milne had a friend at Court. Battenberg, perhaps realising that if blame was going to be apportioned the Admiralty would come off worst, carefully studied Milne's report and found it satisfactory. He noted that the fact that the German ships did escape was due to Troubridge who 'signally failed in carrying out the task assigned to him by his CinC'.[3] Churchill was less sanguine but accepted his First Sea Lord's verdict. Milne was told, 'Your general dispositions and the measures taken by you ... are fully approved by their Lordships,' and that the escape of the *Goeben* was 'due to the failure of Rear Admiral Troubridge to carry out your instructions'. In a private letter to Milne, Battenberg added, 'Having no inkling of Troubridge's misconduct the whole situation was wrapped in mystery ... Looking forward to seeing you tomorrow.'[4]

His Serene Highness Prince Louis of Battenberg, First Sea Lord to Churchill since 1912, had been born a prince of the blood in Graz, Austro Hungary. He was the son of Prince Alexander of Hesse and Rhine and was a German national who became a naturalised British subject. His early career had been furthered by intervention from both Queen Victoria and Edward VII, and his wife Victoria was a granddaughter of the Queen, niece of Edward VII and cousin to George V. He was definitely a 'royal' (although oddly Fisher regarded him as a competent officer). Milne would be familiar to him through Milne's friendship with Edward and Alexandra and his long service on royal yachts. Milne, the royal favourite of two successive monarchs had his protection in place.

The die was cast. A victim had been identified. The coward would be outed.

On 9 September Ernest was recalled to England to face a court of inquiry, to be held at Portsmouth on the 22nd. Una returned with him. The court consisted of two senior Admirals, Callaghan and Meux. Callaghan was old navy and had been in command of the Grand Fleet until the outbreak of war, when Churchill brushed him aside to put Jellicoe in place (he had also served as Commander on the *Bellerophon* during Watson and Troubridge's cruise of 1889–1892). He was hugely respected. At the time he was First and Principal ADC to the King. Meux, fabulously wealthy by way of a legacy from the eccentric and widowed Lady Meux (he changed his name to hers as part of the terms of the bequest) was an intimate of King Edward VII and George V and had been a leading figure in the Beresford faction. He was CinC Portsmouth. They were both navy establishment, royals, traditionalists.

The court confined itself to the question of whether Ernest should have engaged the *Goeben* and it didn't take much time deciding that he should have done so. It did not consider *Goeben* a superior force; it thought that with four cruisers and a faster rate of fire than *Goeben*, the 1st Cruiser Squadron could have fired a greater weight of broadside than the German ship; and that the British ships had a very good chance of at least delaying the *Goeben* or causing her to seek internment in a neutral port. Troubridge's failure to engage was 'deplorable and contrary to the tradition of the British Navy'. Accordingly, Ernest was to face a court martial. The Silver King was to go on trial for his service life

Only two flag officers had been tried by courts martial in the preceding 40 years. Many wanted Troubridge tried for cowardice which could have attracted a most serious penalty. In fact he was tried on the charge that he did 'through negligence or other default, forbear to pursue the chase of His Imperial Majesty's ship *Goeben*, being an enemy then flying.'

Thus, on 5 November, on board HMS *Bulwark* at Portland, Troubridge handed his sword to the president of the court and went on trial for his reputation and career before a court of nine officers, presided over by the CinC Plymouth.

## Cradock

There was to be one further calamity consequent on Troubridge's refusal to accept battle and his subsequent court of inquiry. The loss of Rear Admiral Sir Christopher (Kit) Cradock and over 1600 men of the 4th Cruiser Squadron at the battle of Coronel.

Cradock's mission was to 'seek and destroy' Vice Admiral Graf von Spee, who was roaming the Pacific and Atlantic Oceans. But armed with a weak squadron, Cradock knew he couldn't defeat his superior opponent. Despite his concerns, the Admiralty and Churchill were insistent he follow orders, which seemed to him to give him no chance but to fight. And so, on 1 November 1914 he did so in the certain knowledge that he could not win. Cradock was fully aware of Troubridge's performance in the Mediterranean and the opprobrium it had attracted, both to Ernest personally and to his beloved navy, in which he had served for over 40 years. He was grimly determined that he would not suffer Troubridge's fate and that the Navy's reputation would be protected. In one of his last letters he wrote, 'I am generally pretty lucky and we don't want any more disappointments.' The shadow of Troubridge's presumed cowardice hung over Cradock as he sailed to his death.[5]

# 13

## On Trial, November 1914

A court martial is the ultimate sanction that the armed forces can bring against one of its members. It can break careers, reputations and – in 1914 – even call forth the death sentence for the most heinous offences. Troubridge's reputation and his family's good name rested on the outcome of the trial.

The format does not replicate that of a civil or criminal case. The case is heard by a panel of senior officers, the defence is most often conducted by a friend of the accused and the prosecutor is a naval officer. The court that convened on HMS *Bulwark* on Thursday 5 November under Admiral Sir George Le Clerc Egerton comprised four other admirals and four captains, together with the Deputy Judge Advocate as legal advisor to the panel. Egerton was old navy, had served as Second Sea Lord in 1911 (from which position he was summarily fired by Churchill on becoming First Lord, 'dismissed like a butler' according to Dudley de Chair), was a quondam ADC to King Edward VII and had once had Robert Falcon Scott as his flag-captain.

Ernest might or might not have chosen correctly in the early hours of 7 August, but his touch was much more assured in his choice of an 'Accused's Friend' – in other words, defence counsel – for his trial. Leslie F. Scott KC, MP (later Sir Leslie) had attended New College, Oxford, taken silk in 1909 and had been elected MP for Liverpool Exchange in 1910 (a seat he would hold until 1922). He specialised in commercial and international maritime law and had represented the British government at maritime law conferences in Brussels in 1909 and 1910. Forty-five years old at the time of the court martial, he was regarded as an outstanding barrister and a formidable opponent in court, an opinion justified after the war when he became Solicitor-General in 1922 and Lord Justice of Appeal from 1935 to 1948. He was supported by a solicitor, Sir Henry Jackson. This was a high-class defence team but also a high-cost one. Ernest was clearly bent on protecting his reputation at all costs and prepared to pay significant legal expenses to do so.

The prosecutor was, as tradition required, a naval officer, Rear Admiral Sydney Freemantle. He had joined the Admiralty in 1910 as the Head of the War Division, and by 1912 he was at Portsmouth as President of the Signal Committee. While in this role he had been charged with overseeing the overhaul of existing signal systems and books to incorporate the latest advances in wireless telegraphy. His suggestion for a dedicated communications department had been overtaken by the outbreak of war, but in 1914 a Signals Division was established at the Admiralty with Fremantle as its chief and it was from this role that he was seconded to act as prosecutor. He was an intelligent man but neither a trained advocate nor a lawyer.

The court was 'closed' for certain pieces of evidence ('in the interests of the state') but oddly there were no newspaper reporters anyway – none had applied for credentials to attend.

Wray was the first witness but only to swear the ship's log. He was followed by a navigational expert who testified as to the relative positions of all the vessels involved. But what everybody in the public gallery really wanted was to see Milne, for he had after all been 'cleared' by the Admiralty under Battenberg's direction and was thus able to support or decry Ernest's case as he pleased.

The basis of the prosecution's case was twofold. First, Troubridge had repeated orders that *Goeben* was his objective which could only mean that he should attack her. Second, *Goeben* was not a superior force. Milne testified that Ernest should have continued the chase and that the loss of one or two cruisers would have been acceptable; and that at no time had Troubridge stated that his force was not strong enough, a charge Troubridge denied, saying that he had assumed he would have the battle cruisers with him. Ernest himself said that he expected that Milne would return the big ships to him if he encountered the *Goeben* or otherwise shadow the German force with them, rather than leaving it to the 1st Cruiser Squadron. Each blamed the other.

Key to Ernest's defence that *Goeben* represented a superior force was his relating of the advice given by Wray his flag-captain that *Goeben* outranged him and that his 9.2-inch guns would be ineffective above 8000 yards because they were inaccurately calibrated. In this regard it would have no doubt interested the court to have noted that, when *Gloucester* attempted to engage the *Breslau* to slow down the Germans' flight, her 6-inch guns hit the German vessel at 10,000 yards – and that the *Breslau*'s 4.1-inch guns ranged on the *Gloucester* too. But these facts were not brought to the court's attention.

Scott conducted a brilliant defence; he repeatedly clashed with Egerton, asking to see documents that the president refused to disclose, and thus establishing some doubt as to why they were being withheld. He also set out to discredit Milne, making it appear at times as if he, Milne, were on trial rather than Ernest. On the subject of the relative forces disposed, he asked Milne, 'What are the chief elements to enter into the question of relative force?' to which Milne replied, 'Gun power, weather and speed. I do not know of anything else.'[1] (So armour accounted for nothing, a point which, amazingly, neither Scott nor the court picked up.) Scott was thus able to introduce evidence concerning the *Goeben*'s superior range of fire from Admiral Sir Percy Scott, the navy's leading gunnery expert as to the relative ranges (25,000 yards for the *Goeben*, 16,000 for *Defence* he reckoned) and, although Percy Scott not able to attend in person and therefore this was not allowed as evidence, the opinion carried weight. The defining moment of the defence was when Leslie Scott requested Milne to show on a chart how Troubridge should have manoeuvred his ships to engage *Goeben* without being sunk himself. Scott had rehearsed these tactics with some officers beforehand and no one had solved the problem. Milne prevaricated. At this point Counsel clashed with Egerton again who – effectively – said that

Milne was not on trial and did not need to answer this question. But Scott kept hounding him and Milne's evidence dragged into a second day, its overwhelming characteristic being waffle and a steadfast refusal to offer any support to Troubridge. Scott now changed tack and started to pursue the thought that Milne was actually at fault for the *Goeben's* escape as he kept the battle cruisers with him, did not cut Souchon off in the Medina Straits and was slow in reinforcing Troubridge's squadron. Once again Egerton reminded him that Milne was not on trial. Wray was now re-called to give his evidence. He reiterated his claim that 1st Cruiser Squadron was out-ranged by *Goeben* and testified as to Ernest's distress at calling off the fight.

It was now Troubridge's turn to give evidence; but it was 5 pm on Saturday and the court instead adjourned until Monday morning, the 9th. Ernest, no doubt, spent an uncomfortable weekend considering his fate.

Unlike a civil court, in a court martial the defence is opened not by Counsel but by the Accused. Ernest therefore gave a peroration of some length in which he lucidly set out his case and his feelings at the time. The language was skilfully chosen, and might owe more to Scott's drafting than Ernest's own prose. It made much of the definition of 'superior force' and how much more difficult the choice was to refuse rather than accept battle when confronted with the circumstances that prevailed on 6/7 August. Again he focused on the *Goeben's* ability to outrange his four ships and pick them off one by one. With admirable sophistry, he went on to argue (when pressed as to why he forbore to chase the *Goeben*) that he had no right to put himself into a position where he was likely to engage a superior force while he had it in his power to avoid being brought to action. What ever happened to the spirit of Nelson?

Ernest had begun his evidence at 0945 and spoke for 70 minutes. It was then time for the cross examination. When asked why he did not continue the chase after he had decided to refuse battle, Troubridge squarely blamed Milne: 'All he had to do was signal three words – continue the chase.'[2]

At 1525 the court withdrew to consider its findings; four hours later it reconvened. The court had clearly been much impressed with Scott's antics. At just after 7.30 in the evening Troubridge entered the court to see his sword on the table, hilt towards him. Egerton returned it to him. He had been found not guilty.

The court's findings were thirteen-fold (see Appendix 6) but the crux and thrust of them were clear. They stated that it appeared the Accused would get no support for the 1st Cruiser Squadron and that from his then position it was impossible for him to attack the *Goeben* before daylight. The ruling recognised that, in view of the instructions he received from the Admiralty, Ernest was justified in considering that he must not abandon his watch on the Adriatic having regard to the transportation of the French troops then taking place between Algeria and France and the possibility of the Austrian Fleet coming out.

The court further opined that, in view of the instruction received from the Admiralty by the Commander-in-Chief and repeated by him in his Sailing Orders to Troubridge, and also the signal made on 4 August that 1st C.S. and *Gloucester* are not to get seriously engaged with a superior force, the court formed the opinion that under the particular circumstances of weather, time and position, Ernest was justified in considering the *Goeben* was a superior force to the 1st C.S. at the time they would have met. The judgement went on to recognise that although it was possible that Troubridge could have brought the *Goeben* to action, in view of his orders to watch the Adriatic he was justified in abandoning the chase at the time he did, as he had no news or prospect of any force being sent to his assistance.

Finally, and as a result of their deliberations, the court found that the charge against Ernest was not proved, and fully and honourably acquitted him of the accusations.

These findings implicitly (and indeed explicitly) criticised the Board of the Admiralty, who were quick to voice their annoyance and disbelief in the verdict. The Silver Fox might have slipped the hounds but the huntsmen were not finished with him yet.

Fisher, reinstalled as First Sea Lord, thought Milne was to blame. Milne 'should have been off Messina himself with his three battle cruisers ... this covers the lesser case of Admiral Troubridge ... [who] was at fault for giving up the chase,'[3] he minuted. Cecil Lambert, Fourth Sea Lord, thought that 'a great blunder has been committed'.

Admiral Tudor, Third Sea Lord, noted that 'the findings of the court martial appear to be correct on the basis of the evidence educed but I am of the opinion that its conclusions are wrong, both from the commonsense point of view and technically.' He added 'that the ships of the 1st Cruiser Squadron stood a chance of being severely punished ... [that it] can be accepted but that they could have been destroyed ... before the *Goeben* had expended her ammunition seems to me to be out of the question.'[4]

Second Sea Lord Hamilton, a royal favourite himself, stated that 'the court has been led off the track by a clever lawyer'. He dismissed Wray's evidence that *Goeben* was a superior force and added that it was a pity the court had not asked him how many *Defence*s he would have needed to engage the *Goeben*; he added that the court seemed to have decided to try Milne rather than Troubridge. He then defended Milne's dispositions (which, of course had been concurred with by the Admiralty) at some length. In his conclusion, Hamilton saved his best vitriol for Wray who 'should remain unemployed as it is decidedly dangerous to have an officer of his opinions in a responsible position'.[5] And finally, old Arthur Wilson, unpaid advisor to the Admiralty board: 'The *Goeben* could no doubt choose her own range but unless German gunnery is very much better than ours she would have to expend all her ammunition before she could put the four ships out of action keeping outside 15,400 yards.'[6]

In a desperate attempt to question the verdict Churchill asked the Judge Advocate of the Fleet to review the findings of the court. On 14 November he reviewed the process of the trial in a memo. His conclusion toed the Admiralty party line; 'the result of the above criticism is that the finding is not what it should be – a complete reasoned statement of all the material facts leading up to an acquittal.'[7] It was flawed, but not enough to overturn the verdict.

After the verdict Troubridge wrote to Bridgeman, a retired First Sea Lord engineered out by Churchill in 1912, 'Good God, what a cruel shame. They say in the fleet that Cradock lost his squadron because Churchill court martialled Troubridge for not losing his.'[8] Ernest retained for ever a dislike of Churchill – whom he viewed as the motivating force behind his arraignment – and was enraged that his 'real accuser' had not been his fellow naval colleagues but 'an amateur'. In this he might have been mistaken, for it was Battenberg who had pressed hardest for his indictment and Churchill followed his lead.

Una thought that Ernest had few supporters in the navy. She wrote that 'Zyp was not over popular with his colleagues. He could be domineering, said what he thought ... was scathing about less able officers.'[9] Few, it seemed, rallied round him in his hour of need.

The opinions of both Ernest's Counsel, Leslie Scott, and the Prosecutor, Freemantle, are instructive. Scott had 'expected an acquittal on the charges as framed but if Troubridge had been tried for vacillation, no counsel could have saved him'. Freemantle wrote that 'the admiralty telegram was badly worded' and that Troubridge 'assumed too readily that *Goeben* was a superior force and magnified the deficiencies of his own ships'.[10]

Ernest might have won a personal battle, but he had lost a personal war. His Lords and Masters were very definitely of the opinion that he was at best incompetent and at worst a coward. And the Admiralty were not going to forgive him lightly, for Churchill and his colleagues were attracting opprobrium and blame on a regular basis. Cradock's loss in the Pacific was being laid at their door by some, and the debacle of the disaster that was the loss of 'Force C' added to their discomfort.

On 22 September three old *Cressy* class armoured cruisers were patrolling off the Dutch coast. They had been, as Battenberg had put it, 'peddling up and down' here since the outbreak of war to keep an eye on possible German light craft activity. Senior naval officers such as Keyes, Tyrwhitt and Jellicoe had argued against the continuance of the patrols as too dangerous. The cruisers were elderly, vulnerable and predictable. Officially called 'Force C', they were known in the navy as 'the live bait squadron'. At 0630 the *Aboukir* was hit by a torpedo from *U9* and sank. The *Hogue* was trying to rescue survivors when she too was hit and sank in 10 minutes. The *Cressy*, which by now should have been running for her life, unbelievably hove to and capsized at 0717 having been hit by two torpedoes. Sixty-two officers and 1397 men (mostly middle-aged reservists and cadets straight out of the Dartmouth naval college) went down with the ships – ships which in any case were of little or no value – but the men were. Keyes, in pleading for the ships to be withdrawn, had had his request dismissed contemptuously by Sturdee (Chief of Staff) telling him that he knew nothing of the history of the Dutch wars (fought in the seventeenth century!) if he did not appreciate the importance of patrolling the 'Broad Fourteens'.

A court of inquiry was set up and found that some blame was attributable to all of the senior officers involved – Captain Drummond (the senior officer present) for not zigzagging and for not calling for destroyers; Rear Admiral Christian (in command on the day but not the force commander, who had to leave his vessels before the encounter to refuel) for not making it clear to Drummond that he could summon destroyers; and Rear Admiral Campbell (the actual force commander) for not being present and for a very poor performance at the enquiry at which he stated that he did not know what the purpose of his command was (both admirals were 'royals' and loathed as such by Fisher). But the bulk of the blame was directed at the Admiralty for persisting with a patrol that was dangerous and of limited value against the advice of senior seagoing officers. Both the Third and Fourth Sea Lords added to the criticism of the conduct of the Admiralty.

This could not have improved the distaste in Admiralty House for the fact that Troubridge had 'got off' the court martial and they, the leaders of navy, had instead been blamed. And now it had happened again.

Nor were the press satisfied with the explanations emanating from the Admiralty. *The Times* fulminated, 'The nation should be told quite frankly how these two blameless Admirals [Troubridge and Milne] came to let the *Goeben* escape, and thus set in motion a series of events of great importance, the end of which no man can forsee.'[11] The paper went on to suggest a cover-up, a plot to conceal the truth.

Henry Fitch, writing much later, commented that 'there has always been a certain stigma attached to the affair'.[12] But perhaps the last word can be left to Henry Horniman: 'Troubridge was found not guilty. I, in common with many others, was never able to understand how such a result came about.'[13]

# 14

## Disgrace; London, November 1914 to January 1915

Milne was told by Churchill that the war had changed things and he could no longer take up the Nore command. He was never to hold any further command at sea or on land, despite repeated protestations of his desire to do so.

Troubridge might have been found not guilty but he too was not offered any further employment at sea. Instead, Ernest was ordered to be discharged to admin duties – which really meant unemployed – and he returned to Una and his home in St George's Square. Throughout the court martial Una had taken to her bed and not stirred from it to support Ernest. By now their marriage was a living lie. The heart had gone out of it and a gulf existed between them, one widened by Una's knowledge that many people in her circle and more generally thought that there was a whiff of disgrace around Ernest. She wrote that 'there were too many incompatibilities between us . . .,' he had made her unhappy, and she 'could not write in defence of her husband'.[1] She offered him no sympathy, feeling that he had inflicted some sort of social stigma on her.

As for their marriage, for her it had perhaps been an attempt to replace her father, which had been bound to misfire. For him, it was 'a marriage of sexual attraction which went sour'.[2] He himself had put on weight and was perhaps not the handsome man he had been. He had a commanding manner and had grown up expecting to be obeyed and indulged. She possibly found intercourse painful because of the salpingitis. There was no love in the marriage for either of them and Ernest could find little succour in this time of need.

However, he did have some friends in high places. Churchill was embarrassed in the House of Lords by a question from Lord Curzon asking why such a senior admiral, honourably acquitted, was not being more usefully employed. Fisher and the Board would not countenance giving him another sea command, and Churchill himself had fallen out with Ernest in 1912 and was not a man to forget a grudge. Then an opportunity presented itself. Serbia – a chance to get Troubridge out of sight and out of mind – and Churchill off the hook. The Serbians, their country battered by the initial Austro-Hungarian assault, desperately needed help, and naval assistance had been requested. On 21 January 1915 Churchill sent for Troubridge. It was one of the strangest interviews of Ernest's life.

When Troubridge was ushered into his office, Churchill continued to write, head down, and refused to acknowledge him for some two minutes. Finally he looked up and fixed Ernest with a glare. Without preamble Churchill said, 'I have an appointment to offer you but as it is in the forefront of battle I think you may not care to accept it.'[3] Taking such a tone to a senior officer was unprecedented. Troubridge blanched; but he swallowed his pride and accepted. Any opportunity to recover his reputation, and prove his bravery, was to be seized. He replied that he was ready to accept any appointment that was useful to his country in time of war.

## Bravery

Vincit omnia virtus *(Courage conquers all)*

Aristotle stated that 'a courageous act does not necessarily make one courageous'. But bravery was nonetheless the default position for the navy. It was expected that a British naval officer, or ordinary sailor, would be brave and courageous, self-sacrificing and gallant. It was part of the self-image of the tribe, the belief system that sustained the navy's values. Old and heroic sailors were accorded mystical respect and reverence; the 'Vicwardian' educational system prized and emphasised the exploits of Nelson, Drake, Jervis, Raleigh and Grenville. Public schools across the land had their 'houses' named after these heroes and more.

Grenville was the exemplar of the breed. Born in Devon in 1542 he fought bravely against the Spanish armada. In 1591 Grenville found himself vice admiral of the fleet under Thomas Howard. Charged with keeping a squadron in the Azores to intercept the Spanish treasure ships, and flying his flag in the galleon *Revenge*, he and Howard were surprised off Flores by a much larger squadron sent by Philip II of Spain. Howard retreated to safety, but Grenville faced the 53 enemy ships alone, leading his single ship in a suicide mission, saying – according to Raleigh – that he 'utterly refused to turn from the enimie ... he would rather chose to die than to dishonour himselfe'. He was short over 100 crewmen because of sickness on shore but he chose to confront the vastly superior Spanish force. All day long he fought the Spanish, causing heavy damage to fifteen galleons. According to Raleigh's account, Grenville and his soldiers fought for hour after hour, 'until all the powder of The *Revenge*, to the last barrell, was now spent, all her pikes broken, fortie of her best men slain, and the most part of the rest hurt'. The ship itself was 'marvellous unsaverie, filled with bloud and bodies of deade and wounded men like a slaughter house'.

In the nineteenth century, poet laureate Alfred Lord Tennyson helped further the legend with his poem 'The Revenge'. 'Out-gunned, out-fought, and out-numbered fifty-three to one', Grenville was made to say that he wished to blow up his ship rather than give up the fight: 'Sink me the ship, Master Gunner—sink her, split her in twain! ... Fall into the hands of God, not into the hands of Spain!' This was the sort of death befitting a British naval officer. The contrast between Grenville's decision and that taken by Troubridge would have been obvious to many people both within and outside the navy, especially those who had benefited from a Victorian education.

Horatio Nelson was another naval hero who had attained near deification even before the Battle of Trafalgar. Following his death at sea popular mourning was widespread and near hysterical, and monuments and paintings of him sprang up all over Britain and the Colonies. His dictum 'no captain can do wrong who lays his ship alongside the enemy' became a sort of shorthand of British naval strategy. In the 1860s Tennyson appealed to the image and tradition of Nelson, in order to oppose the defence cuts being made by Prime Minister Gladstone. Jackie Fisher revered him and was always quoting his aphorisms. Churchill took great inspiration from his exploits. His successes were the staple of public school history lessons.

More recent deeds of valour made the fame and careers of many Vicwardian sailors. Old 'Ard 'Eart – Admiral Sir Arthur Wilson, a quondam First Sea Lord – won the Victoria Cross as a captain in the Mahdist Wars when in 1884 he singlehandedly held off an attack while his crew brought a jammed heavy machine gun back into action. The then Commander Christopher Cradock won fame and promotion to Captain through his deeds on land in the Boxer rebellion of 1900. Trying to restart a stalled attack by a mixed force he exposed himself to a rain of enemy fire with a fine disregard for his personal safety. He later wrote, 'I felt that, if nothing else, I was doing my duty and upholding our great country's traditions by the example our men set to the foreigners.'⁴ In the same campaign, John Jellicoe – later to command the Grand Fleet – was badly wounded at the Battle of Beicang and told he would die. He confounded medical opinion by showing a typically naval disregard for such nonsense and lived to the age of seventy-six. And again, in the Boxer fighting, an eighteen-year-old midshipman (later Commander) Basil John Douglas Guy, serving in the Naval Brigade, won the Victoria Cross for his bravery in attempting to rescue a fallen sailor. His citation, as printed in *The London Gazette*, read:

On 13th July 1900, during the attack on Tientsin City, a very heavy cross-fire was brought to bear on the Naval Brigade, and there were several casualties. Among those who fell was an able seaman, shot about 50 yards short of cover. Mr Guy stopped with him, and, after seeing what the injury was, attempted to lift him up and carry him in, but was not strong enough, so after binding up the wound Mr Guy ran to get assistance. In the meantime, the remainder of the company had passed in under cover, and the entire fire from the city wall was concentrated on Mr Guy and the other man. Shortly after Mr Guy had got in under cover the stretchers came up, and again Mr Guy dashed out and assisted in placing the wounded man on the stretcher and carrying him in. The wounded man was however shot dead just as he was being carried into safety. During the whole time, a very heavy fire had been brought to bear upon Mr Guy, and the ground around him was absolutely ploughed up.[5]

This description sums up the total of the expectations from a British naval officer – valour, self-sacrifice, chivalry, gallantry. And these were the qualities that many people now believed Ernest lacked.

Before taking up his new post Troubridge was approached by Fawcett Wray, now also unemployed (he had been relieved of command of *Defence* on 5 October 1914, a month after Ernest's recall), who wished Troubridge to influence Churchill to exculpate him (Wray) from the cloud of cowardice that hung over him too. Troubridge now began a subtle rewriting of history himself. According to Wray's later account he stated that he would have fought the *Goeben* if it hadn't been for Wray. When Wray then asked how he reconciled this with his evidence at the court martial, Troubridge responded, 'My dear Wray, by the time you are an Admiral and have a staff of your own you will realise that you must be true to your staff. I did that to save you.'[6] In such ways is history manufactured.

And so, at the end of the month, dressed in the uniform of a Serbian general (for the Serbian troops tended to shoot at any unfamiliar dress), Ernest set off for the Balkans as head of the British Naval Mission to Serbia and his headquarters on the Danube. He was not completely without his supporters. The right-wing editor of the *National Review*, Leo Maxse, wrote to him on his departure, 'We must stand by Serbia ... your presence there, however inadequately supported, will be of the greatest value.'[7] With this statement Maxse was reflecting a growing body of opinion in England which had been fanned by the Serbs' own energetic recruiting, fundraising and propagandising, spearheaded by Madame Grouitch, the American wife of Dr Slavko Grouitch a senior Serb diplomat. It had become the done thing to support 'gallant little Serbia', even more so because Serbia was the only member of the Allies against the Central Powers which had enjoyed any military success. It was increasingly and conveniently forgotten that it was the Serb-inspired assassination of Archduke Franz Ferdinand at Sarajevo on 28 June 1914 which had triggered the conflict in the first place. The general view previously pertaining, as expressed by Prime Minister Asquith to the Archbishop of Canterbury, was that the Serbs deserved a thorough thrashing.

Una went with Ernest but soon returned and devoted herself to raising funds and nursing volunteers for a hospital there for British servicemen. This project was complete by September and the Admiralty offered her passage with the nurses back to Belgrade. But the prospect depressed her and she stayed behind.

# 15

## John, London, 1915

'John' was Marguerite Antonia Radclyffe-Hall, the second child of Radclyffe Radclyffe-Hall (also known as 'Rat') and Mary (Marie) Jane Sager, born on 12 August 1880 at West Cliff, Bournemouth. She was an only child, her sister having died in infancy.

Her mother, an American widow, had married the extravagant and priapic Radclyffe, grandson of a wealthy and knighted Lancashire physician who had made a large fortune from sanatoria. Unsuited to the demands of domestic life, he left his new wife months before Marguerite was born. Marguerite's parents divorced three years after her birth. According to her biographer, Michael Baker 'she rarely saw her father thereafter and was unloved by her volatile mother, who remarried in 1890'.[1] Her mother's new husband was Alberto Visetti, a professor of singing at the Royal College of Music.

Marguerite showed a precocious musical talent but apparently received little encouragement from her stepfather (although he did, it is suggested, make sexual advances towards her). Her education was fitful and she remained a chronic bad speller all her life. She was a restless child and alongside her interest in music, particularly the piano, she composed lyrics (later collected in five volumes of poetry), enjoyed pets (her only friends in a loveless London childhood home), horses, riding and motor cars, all the while pursuing attachments to girls and young women, none of which suited her socially ambitious mother who longed to find her a socially advantageous match.

Hall's first serious romantic attachment was to a singer called

Agnes Nicholls, who boarded with her mother. After she came of age, Hall visited her American relatives and developed close friendships with her cousins Jane Randolph and Dorothy Diehl. Hall claimed that she was never in the slightest attracted to men.

In 1901, at the age of twenty-one, she inherited a very large sum of money which had been left in trust by her grandfather Charles Radclyffe-Hall. This allowed her complete freedom in her life and she decided to become a writer. She started to travel widely, including America, France, Italy and Germany. Aged twenty-eight and visiting Germany and the spa of Bad Homberg she met, and then lived with, the singer Mabel Veronica Batten (known as 'Ladye') who was twenty-five years her senior. Mabel was a noted beauty, had been painted by John Singer Sergeant and was married to George Batten. They initially formed a *ménage à trois* until Mabel left her husband to live with Marguerite, and the relationship continued until Ladye's death in 1916.

Around the time of the start of this liaison, Marguerite 'came out' as an overt lesbian. According to Baker, 'Believing herself a man trapped in a woman's body, she liked to be called John, assumed a male pseudonym, and cultivated a strikingly masculine appearance, sporting cropped hair, bow-ties, smoking jackets, and pipes.'[2]

Ladye was cousin to Una Troubridge and in August 1915, at a party in London, Ladye introduced 'John' to Una. It was to be a fateful event. They shared an interest in psychic research and the paranormal (as well as animals). Una, a recognised artist, and Marguerite the aspiring writer, seventeen years older, a woman but one with the forceful characteristics of a dominant man, got on well. John told Una that she wanted to bed her; and on 29 November 1915, in Malvern, they became lovers. It was the start of a relationship that would last until John's death 28 years later.

## Lesbianism

Although George V was on the throne there was no new Georgian culture. Attitudes were generally governed by the mores of the Victorian and Edwardian ages and nowhere more so than in matters sexual. Attitudes towards homosexuality were confused. On the one hand, the cult of male sexual attraction was well known and – it might be argued – even promoted in the many public schools and in universities as a sort of brotherhood or cultural statement, an aestheticism of higher appreciation. In this the Vicwardians followed their heroes the ancient Greeks, who regarded male on male love and sex as superior intellectually and physically to that of a man and a woman. On the other hand, those caught openly practising homosexuality in a public setting were severely punished and their reputations shredded. The destruction of artists such as Oscar Wilde or Simeon Solomon and the flight and exile of Lord Arthur Somerset serve as examples of the many. Sodomy had been a capital offence until 1861 and remained an underground activity whose practitioners were generally regarded with unease and lived in fear of exposure.

Lesbianism was hardly recognised. That lesbianism existed in ancient times was just about understood (the word itself derives from the poems of Sappho, poet of Lesbos, and her works were accepted because they were of the ancient Greek canon); but that there were such people alive in the world of 1915 was barely comprehended. It was recognised that women appreciated the company of other women and that single, spinster or widowed women would live together for company. But sexual relations between females were not acknowledged publicly and if discussed at all it was with fear and contempt. This despite the fact that the ancient Greeks – so adored by the Vicwardians – accepted that their womenfolk were enthusiastic users of dildos, made of wood or padded leather, liberally anointed with olive oil and called *olisbos*. The Greek word for female homosexuals was *Tribads* and tribadism even then was used as a term of abuse. Athenians believed that Sparta (their traditional enemy) was a hotbed of tribadism and Plutarch recorded that 'at Sparta love was held in such honour that even the most respectable women became infatuated with girls'.

Sappho, who ran an academy for girls on the island of Lesbos, dedicated her verse to the girls she taught. Apuleius called it 'wanton' and 'sensual', Ovid described her oeuvre as a complete course in female homosexuality. But that was history; lesbianism was neither seen nor heard in the polite society of the early twentieth century. Nonetheless there was a lesbian sub-culture at work, its existence due to true single sex attraction as well as the need in such a stultifying culture to 'kick against the traces' and individualise oneself by adopting counter-cultural mores.

Science too began to take a tentative interest. At the very end of the nineteenth century questions of sexual identity were the subject of pseudo-scientific investigation, dubbed sexology. Writers such as Havelock Ellis attempted a detailed classification of 'normal' and 'perverse' sexual practices. This led to the identification of a 'third' or 'intermediate' sex, for which Ellis used the term 'sexual inversion'. Marguerite later adopted this term to describe her own psychology. Ellis himself married as a virgin and late (at 32), and took as his bride a practising lesbian. At the turn of the century lesbian and Sapphic came to be accepted as terms for female relationships.

Criminalisation of female homosexuality was planned in 1885 but the plan was dropped, apocryphally because Queen Victoria said that such things could not exist and declined to sign the bill. Gentlemen whose wives were suspected of lesbianism were made a laughing stock, deemed incapable of keeping their wives under control or of satisfying their needs. Although male homosexuality remained illegal, female same-sex relationships were not recognised by statute and therefore, although morally discouraged, were not illegal. The nearest 'case' that might be constructed legally against lesbians was that of being an 'unchaste woman'. In an historical context this was anomalous as there had been laws in place against female on female sex in France since 1270. In Spain, Italy, and the Holy Roman Empire, sodomy between women was included in acts considered unnatural and punishable by burning to death, although few instances are recorded of this taking place.

However, from the seventeenth to the nineteenth centuries a woman expressing passionate love for another woman was fashionable, accepted, and encouraged. These *soi disant* romantic friendships were common in England and there is a large body of documentation in the volumes of letters written between women. Whether these relationships included any sexual component is less clear but women could form strong and exclusive bonds with each other and still be considered virtuous; a similar relationship with a man would have destroyed a woman's reputation. In fact, these relationships were promoted as alternatives to, and possibly practice for, a woman's marriage to a man. After the Great War, and in the context of a lack of available men due to the slaughter of the trenches, cohabiting women became commonplace and accepted.

But for a woman to usurp a man's role in a relationship, for a woman to turn seducer and overtly take on manly traits and character, for there to be a sexual component in the relationship between a woman and another woman – this was considered beyond the pale. Such behaviour was immoral, corrupting, against the natural order of things and to be severely censured. Loss of reputation befell anyone so accused and such accusations had been used to undermine the authority of prominent women including *inter alia* Marie Antoinette of France, Queen Anne, Sarah Churchill, Duchess of Marlborough, and Queen Christina of Sweden.

Una and John would have been aware that there were artistic role models for their proclivities. The poets Katherine Bradley and her niece Edith Cooper, who wrote collaboratively from the 1880s under the name Michael Field, and the Irish writers Edith Somerville and Violet Martin, were known to be lesbian. The Victorian painters Rosa Bonheur, who declined to hide her leanings and was well known for her openly 'masculine' freedom and demeanour, and her live-in lover Anne Klumpke were other exemplars. The composer Ethyl Smyth ('large, aggressive and dressed in manly tweeds'[3]) made no secret of her leanings and professed her love for her fellow suffragette Emmeline Pankhurst, whose daughter Christabel lived for a time in a *ménage à trois* with Eva Gore-Booth (sister of Constance the Irish nationalist agitator) and Esther Roper, who lived openly together as a couple and founded the radical journal *Urania* which expressed their views on gender and sexuality

And then there was the Victorian novelist and poet, the high priest of Victorian romanticism, Henry Newbolt, he of 'Vitai Lampada' fame ('There's a breathless hush in the close tonight, ten to make and the match to win') who married Margaret Duckworth, a woman of charm but somewhat mannish character. She rode to hounds at a furious pace, was as interested in science as in music and defied her religious mother by studying Darwinian biology. Margaret was already in love with her cousin, the beautiful Ella Coltman, with whom she had a long-term lesbian relationship. They were both members of the Grecians, a club of women who studied Greek poetry, abjured the company of men, and privately gave each other male names drawn from the classics. Margaret told Henry she would marry only if Ella became part of their intimate life together and continued as her lover. The threesome did everything in company, Ella even going with them on their honeymoon, but she began to feel left out. So Newbolt solved the problem by taking her as his mistress, while she and Margaret continued as lovers too. Newbolt eventually died at Ella's Kensington house in 1938.

As ever, homosexuality was used as a nationalistic term of abuse. The French called it the 'German vice' (the 'English vice' was flagellation); the English called lesbianism the 'French vice'. So it was this shadow world of the demi-monde that Una entered with John as her guide and companion. And for Ernest, to the taint of the *Goeben* affair was added the social odium of marital scandal.

# 16

## Serbia, 1915–1916

Troubridge and his personal suite took a gentle passage to Belgrade.
He took with him his personal coxswain and attendant, Petty Officer
Newman,[1] his personal servant, Private Davidson RM, and his
secretary, Paymaster Lieutenant Commander Henry Maldon Fitch,
once of the *Defence*. Fitch had been ordered to report to Ernest in
London after Troubridge had selected him from a list of forty
candidates, of which he was the most junior. When Fitch asked why
he had been chosen, Ernest replied, 'Not for your brains but
because you bobbed up in every sport the flag-ship had a hand in. I
always seemed to be giving you medals.'[2] The appointment meant a
double jump in rank for Fitch.

They sailed on 30 January at 1400 aboard the P&O liner *Cale-
donia*. That night they were inoculated against typhoid fever. As
travelling companions they had contingents of soldiers and sailors,
and a sporting rivalry soon developed between the two services. A
game of deck cricket was organised between army and navy, Ernest
captaining the latter. He was bowled first ball by a general, which did
not do much for inter-service relations.

Malta was reached on 7 February and Troubridge went to dinner
with Captain Sowerby, who commanded HMS *Indefatigable*. Ernest
seemed in no hurry to reach Serbia. On the 8th he lunched with
Mrs Carden, wife of the admiral who commanded in the Eastern
Med (and had previously been Admiral Superintendent of the Malta
dockyard), played golf with his flag-lieutenant and dined with a
Mrs Secombe. The following day he called on the French Admiral
Boué de Laperyere, who had commanded French forces during the

*Goeben* affair, lunched with the British consul and played golf. The 10th saw him photographed and lunching with Sowerby on board ship, the 11th lunch with Admiral Carden, and finally on the 13th they embarked for Salonika, arriving on 22 February.

Troubridge's position a vis-à-vis the *Danube* flotilla was never clarified. Although Head of the Naval Mission, he was nonetheless not in command; but the Senior Naval Officer had to act 'in accordance with his wishes'. This was hardly an ideal operational arrangement and Ernest was required to use his diplomatic skills to assert his authority. However, his demeanour made a good impression on the Serbs themselves, and especially on the Crown Prince who acted as Commander in Chief, which allowed him a degree of latitude in his disposition and deployments. Ernest's cultivating of Crown Prince Aleksander had echoes of George about it. Aleksander – young (26 years old), slight, wearing a pince-nez and a small moustache, in Swiss exile for much of his life, rather aloof, nervous, shy and suspicious of the motives of many of those around him – found comfort in the tall, imposing (although increasingly corpulent), shock-haired and confident Troubridge. He took solace in Ernest's bluff Englishness and came increasingly to regard him as a father figure.

This good impression was not shared by all who worked with Troubridge. Captain Vernon Haggard, who served with him on the Danube, penned this portrait:

> He was a queer fellow and I can't pretend I liked him. He had a heavy handsome face with a shock of fine, snowy hair on which he was always using a pocket comb. He was a born poser, had undoubted personality, was a man of the world and had always made his presence felt. But I could not trust him. Whatever he may have been before the *Goeben* and *Breslau* incident, he was now all out for himself and his own interests.[3]

As his Senior Naval Officer Troubridge inherited a commander, Hubert Cardale, who had been in post since October 1914. He also had a mining and torpedo detachment, sent from Malta, of some 27 Royal Marines under a Captain Elliot. The French, also present in limited numbers, had sent one Lieutenant Picot with three 140-mm (5.5-inch) naval guns, and agreed to serve under Ernest; the Russians, with 70 men commanded by Lieutenant Volkovitsy, agreed to talk to him!

The Admiralty had already decided to strengthen the naval forces present by sending a battery of eight 4.7-inch naval guns on travelling mountings together with a detachment of 25 ratings and two officers. The guns arrived a few days after Ernest, commanded by Lieutenant-Commander Charles Kerr, an officer who had been invalided out of the submarine service because of short-sightedness, an affliction which would also seem to ill-fit him for command of a long-range artillery battery. The guns had arrived intact – but minus their sights, rendering them less than effective. In company with this small force had arrived a naval doctor, Surgeon-Lieutenant Merewether, who joined Troubridge's burgeoning staff, as did an engineer, George Bullock, who had been serving in the Serbian army and was now attached to Elliot's party.

In riverine opposition to this small detachment was the Austro-Hungarian Danube River force of six monitors (shallow draft vessels carrying heavy calibre 120-mm guns) and six patrol boats together with a significant artillery presence focused on Belgrade itself.

Troubridge's posting to Serbia had been an elegant solution to Churchill's problem; it successfully got him out of the way and swept under the carpet but it had some unintended consequences. The choice of such a high ranking officer puzzled the French who saw in it some dastardly British plan to curry Serbian favour and – after a successful conclusion of the war with Serbia having gained an Adriatic coast – to be in prime position to sell ships and expertise to a nascent navy. The Serbs on the other hand were delighted and thought it reflected prestige on them and signalled the potential for significant support and supplies; in this they were to be sadly disappointed. But Ernest, always a talented linguist, set himself to learn the Serbian language and built a good working relationship with the army chiefs in Belgrade and at the arsenal town of Kraguevatz. He deployed his guns in static positions commanding the approach to Belgrade and liaised with the French and Russians to ensure coordinated fields of fire. But early 1915 saw little in the way of action. The Austrians, having been beaten off in 1914, were biding their time and an epidemic of typhus was raging throughout Serbia, a good excuse for commanders on both sides to defer action. Typhus, once known as jail fever, is carried by lice and Ernest and his men resorted to tying up their tunic sleeves and trouser bottoms to try to prevent the lice gaining access to their flesh.

Two weeks after his arrival, Ernest had sent a requisition to the Admiralty for a variety of warlike stores; but he also requested a hospital unit to care for his men (and the Serbs), perhaps prompted by the typhus epidemic. The admiralty declined his request; they expressed the view that he already had a medical officer and that would suffice. What followed portrays both Una and Ernest in a favourable light and shows that they were at this stage still acting in concert, at least in public. Stymied by the Admiralty, Ernest asked Una to arrange for medical support to be obtained voluntarily via the Red Cross. Accordingly she set about making arrangements. Within a few weeks she had raised sufficient funds by voluntary subscription and assembled a team. As chief surgeon she recruited Sir Alexander Ogston, an elderly but respected surgeon and bacteriologist, with one other surgeon, a physician, two administrators, a matron, seven nurses, of whom three were VAD (Voluntary Aid Detachment, i.e. nursing auxiliaries) and three male orderlies. They were shipped out in September and installed in an empty school near Troubridge's headquarters but, as observed in Chapter 14, Una declined to accompany them.

It should be noted, however, that supporting Serbia had become a fashionable occupation in Britain. Lady Wimborne, daughter of the 7th Duke of Marlborough and aunt to Winston Churchill, and Lady Paget (at the age of 75) were among several aristocratic ladies who travelled to Serbia to join medical volunteer units in the country; and

Sir Thomas Lipton, 'The King's Grocer' and famous yachtsman, sailed his steam yacht *Erin* to Salonika and then toured Serbian hospitals giving cheer to the inmates. Indeed he visited Ernest's naval 'hospital' in the spring of 1915. It may be that Una had more than half an eye on the views of polite society in her efforts to found the 'Troubridge hospital'.

Churchill and Fisher were keen to invest further resources in opening up the Danube as a means of supporting Serbia and putting pressure on Austria by sending large numbers of troops, but Ernest was not encouraging. There were very few lighters or tugs available. The railways were inadequate for the transportation of troops, and the Serbian army itself was living hand to mouth with no further supplies to spare. This was not necessarily the message that the Admiralty wanted to hear and once more a strain was put on Ernest's reputation for courage. With regard to the alternative of sending troops straight up the Danube, Troubridge was even less enamoured. He needed monitors, torpedo boats and transport ships to make it safe for passage. He did not receive them.

Cardale had previously recommended that they should obtain a powered craft capable of being used to drop torpedoes and in March the Admiralty deigned to send a picket boat (a small, steam-powered launch generally used for communication and tranship-ment purposes in harbour) from Malta, by an overland route. This was fitted out with torpedo equipment and on 23 April Kerr took it on a first offensive mission. Sailing by night he launched torpedoes at an Austrian monitor, thought to be the *Koros*, heard an explosion and thought he had sunk it. Troubridge, watching from Belgrade, saw the explosion and wrote immediately to the Admiralty claiming a first offensive success for him and his forces. Alas, it later tran-spired that the target had been a dummy of canvas and wood. No monitor had after all been destroyed by Kerr and his little ship (which was eventually sunk by artillery fire in July). And still Ernest could not claim to have led a successful action. (Kerr was awarded the DSO for his actions that night.)

Ernest had repeatedly asked the Admiralty for more river vessels but none was forthcoming; so he set about building his own. Local boat builders were asked to construct vessels of a similar design to the picket boat, each to carry a gun, searchlight and torpedoes at a top speed of 15 knots. Three were laid down and in September he wrote to the Admiralty asking for boilers and engines for them. Again, no support was forthcoming; Ernest might have been a rear admiral but he was in a naval backwater and his influence in the corridors of power was nil.

Despite the unfavourable circumstances of his mission, by July Troubridge and his small detachment had effectively sealed the river and established a choke point that prevented the Turks and Bulgarians shipping food, supplies and men to Austria and the Western Front and the Germans from sending equipment and men to reinforce the Turkish defence of the Dardanelles. Likewise the holding of the capital denied the enemy use of the important trans-European railway which passed through both Belgrade and Nis. If Belgrade was well defended Troubridge could continue to hold this position for some time and to great benefit. The Austrians were preparing a response, gathering pontoons behind the river islands out of direct view from the shore but easily observed by his riverine patrols; a bridging attempt was in prospect. Anticipating enveloping attacks, from west and east, he laid plans to deploy his forces upstream and downstream to break these up. Torpedoes could be fired at, and mines floated down against, the pontoon bridge; his naval artillery could add to the attackers' problems and a well-supported defence could create mayhem in the Austrian ranks.

However, he came to understand that this was not the Serbs' preferred strategy. They wanted to draw the Austrians into the country and away from their supply lines and had come to a strategic decision to evacuate Belgrade, and to mount no strong defence there. During the summer men, guns and French spotter aircraft were moved south to the Bulgarian frontier, Serbia's most recent foe and still smarting from the impact of the Treaty of Bucharest, leaving only 6,000 regular Serb troops, some peasant soldiers and the tiny Allied contingents to defend the city. Troubridge was highly critical of this strategy and reported as much to the Admiralty. To be driven off, relieving the choke point, could have impact well beyond the immediate local setback and possibly open the way to Constantinople for the Central Powers. The Serbs paid no heed. In essence this was a conflict of priorities, the Allies being keen to protect the access to the Dardanelles and Constantinople (and hence the Black Sea), the Serbs caring more about preventing the Bulgarians overrunning the south of Serbia and in drawing Austria into an unfavourable position; for this they were prepared to sacrifice their capital. Ernest's imprecations on behalf of the Allied Powers had no effect.

## The Destruction of Serbia

Serbia had bested the Austro-Hungarian invading army in 1914 and thrown them onto the defensive. In order to rectify this embarrassment, a combined German and Austrian army was placed under the command of one of Germany's most able soldiers, Field Marshall August von Mackensen, and a pact agreed between the two Teutonic nations and the Slavs of Bulgaria on 6 September 1915 took as its goal the annihilation of Serbia as a nation state. And so, on 5 October, 470 guns commenced shelling Belgrade from across the Danube and an army of 400,000 men readied themselves to fight.

Serbia was doomed from this moment. Within three days Belgrade had fallen and the Serbian army streamed south in defeat. Five days later the Bulgarian army crossed into Macedonia and South Serbia and the Austro-Hungarians marched in from Dalmatia. By early November the Serbs had retreated to Kosovo, 'the field of Blackbirds', the scene of the defeat by the Turks of the mediaeval Serb Kingdom in 1389, the great mythscape of Serbian nationalism.

Here Crown Prince Aleksander, the Serbian Regent and titular leader in the field, had to decide his course of action. Should he create a new modern Serbian myth with a last desperate stand at Kosovo? Advised by a trio of septuagenarians – his father ex-King Petar, Putnik, the ill (and getting steadily worse) military commander and prime minister Pasic – and consulting Troubridge, who he had asked to join his staff, he recognised the futility of such a sacrifice. The Serb army was ordered to destroy all heavy weaponry and ammunition, gather up thousands of Austrian prisoners and hundreds of horses and oxen and begin the trek over the Prokletije (the Accursed Mountains) into Albania.

Troubridge and the British Naval Mission then faced an epic trek over the mountains, together with hundreds of thousands of Serbian soldiers, to reach safety in Albania and thence evacuation to Corfu. They departed, as part of an advance party of headquarters troops, on 25 November. It was a dreadful journey in shocking winter conditions, made worse by the attentions of Albanian raiders who were intent on settling old scores from the first Balkan War when Serbs had committed atrocities against the Kosovar and Macedonian Albanians.

Survivors of the march compared it to the story of the Grande Armée's withdrawal from Moscow. The tracks the starving army followed through the snow-covered mountains were marked by a trail of corpses. Austrian prisoners and Serbian civilians were mixed haphazard with the disorganised Serb army. The banks of the river Skumbi were littered with the corpses of men, women and children, refugees from Belgrade, whose strength had failed in the crossing. They lay there until their bodies were devoured by dogs.

Without any food for days on end the long files of refugees and a shattered army plodded on through rain and snow over precipitous goat-tracks and through waist-deep marshes. Often they had to turn and drive off attacks from the native Albanians, and some preferred a quick death by their own hand or by falling into a fatal sleep of total exhaustion in the snow, rather than continue to face such sufferings. Of the more than 200,000 men who set out, over 60,000 were to perish. Troubridge later commented to an American reporter, 'I am a big strong man. I can walk without difficulty for days and nights on end but even I felt severely the long drawn-out hardships of that terrible march.'[4]

In fact he was somewhat lucky to survive the trek unscathed; 27 November was a particularly difficult day for Troubridge. He and his small party had to make a steep ascent through four feet of snow and narrow paths barely three feet wide. At one point he became separated from his group and got lost, missed his footing and fell twenty feet downhill, rolling as he went and nearly breaking his leg. Eventually regaining safety and accommodation in a small house, he awoke in the middle of the night, swung his legs out of bed and fell through the floorboards, banging his chin and almost biting off his tongue. He was badly bruised; by morning he felt terrible and 'I simply could not get up at eight, feeling bad.'[5]

After a six-day trek, Ernest finally arrived at the town of Scutari, where the Serbs were establishing an armed camp, and then set forth for the port of San Giovanni di Medua where in December and January 1916, at the personal request of the Crown Prince, he took command of organising the naval evacuation. Given dictatorial authority over the port (which boasted one jetty, a dozen houses and a harbour master's office) and commanding a force of 3,000 Serbian soldiers, he undertook the task of getting foodstuffs (belatedly provided by the British government) unloaded from the waiting ships and transported to the camps inland. Operating from a ruined house near the quayside, he established hygiene and police services and a secure perimeter. He confided to his journal on 20 December that 'I have this morning established myself as Governor of Medua.'[6] This came at a cost however, for Ernest was forced to use his own money to purchase the necessary shelter, beds and food for his men and regularly complained in his diary of the amount of money owed to him by the Admiralty.

Fighting off the threats of marauding Austrian aircraft and epidemic disease, he was then able to successfully complete the evacuation of Allied nationals, the Serbian government-in-exile and the Montenegrin royal family in food ships or Allied destroyers as well as ensuring a steady flow of foodstuffs overland to the camp at Scutari.

His intimacy with the Crown Prince continued (on 17 December his journal entry baldly read 'Dined with the Crown Prince – he handed me the Grand Cross of the Order of the White Eagle').[7] But now Prince Aleksander asked him to embark the remaining men of the Serbian army, some 150,000 strong. This Troubridge refused, arguing that the port facilities were simply inadequate and the risk of enemy attack (their bases were only 60 miles away) on such a large troop movement too high. Durrazo, a southwards march down the coast, was his preference. This set him at odds with the French General Mondesir, who had been given the authority to organise the evacuation. A brisk exchange of views and letters followed, with Troubridge stating that, while he would assist the general by all means in his power he 'declined to take any responsibility for it as it was undertaken against my counsel'.[8] In his journal he noted 'Either I am crazy or everybody else is ... embarking of nearly 100,000 men and 10,000 horses within 40 miles of the enemy's port.'[9] Eventually he prevailed upon the Serbs to accept his advice; just in time, for the Austrians broke through from Montenegro and reached San Giovanni just days after the troops had started for the south and saved themselves from certain destruction.

The Serbian troops marched south to Durrazo and Valona (a port even further south) but – in an action which had echoes of his departure from Japan before the task was complete – Troubridge did not go with them. On 17 January he had an interview with the Crown Prince at which Aleksander asked him to remain with the army so that he could continue to obtain Ernest's advice. Troubridge felt that in such a role he would clash with General Mondesir, to whom he appears to have developed a strong antipathy, and declined (he described Mondesir in his journal as 'a foolish and choleric old man who ought not to be at large' and as 'that stupid old French general').[10] And so on 19 January 1916 Troubridge and his suite boarded an Italian destroyer (the *Schiaffino*). Landing at Brindisi he was transported to the decks of HMS *Queen*, his old command in 1907/8. The crew turned out in force to cheer and applaud him aboard – 'it fairly staggered me' he wrote later.[11] For a man used to disapprobation and neglect from the powers that be, it must have been a fine fillip. Thence to London by way of Rome; and in February he reported for duty at HMS *President* in London.

Meanwhile the remnants of the Serbian army staggered to safety. The survivors who reached Corfu, 155,000 in total, were so emaciated that the hospital nurses could lift them in their arms as if they were babies.

Ernest kept a journal of his time in the Balkans. It reveals that while the Serbs might have been impressed by him, he was not so taken with them. Although initially sympathetic to the country's plight ('Poor little Serbia; I trust we shall be in time to save her but doubt it'), his writings display a man deeply resentful of his circumstances and of those around him. Throughout the days from October 1915 to January 1916, Troubridge does not miss an opportunity to vent his frustration and anger at perceived Serbian duplicity and cowardice, and at his own material discomforts. He dismisses Serbian reports that they are outnumbered and outgunned as an excuse for surrender. As he writes, this was ' … a preparation for chucking up the sponge'.[12] He interprets the Serbian response to the German/ Bulgarian offensive as typical of Slavic incompetence and lack of organisational skill. He writes, 'The Serbs have no organisation in peace so what it is in this emergency can be imagined. It seems to me all are tired of effort, like all Slavs, & wish it was all over & they could resume their normal Slav existence of idleness, plotting & dreaming while the virile Teuton colonises the country, bringing prosperity in his train.'[13] Not being included in the high circles of Serbia's elite, Troubridge denounces the arrogance and privileges enjoyed by this group, while he, his servants and his baggage were not given the same status. He is particularly critical of the General Staff, who steal his carriages to provide transport for their wives ('they have stolen my carriages and baggage') and only seem interested in escaping with their possessions and families. His baggage is scattered to the four winds and he is left with only one trunk ('some Bulgarian is wearing my uniform').[14]

Ernest's *amour propre* is badly offended by the Serbian General Staff's lack of respect for him and his rank. He rails at the Serbian chief of staff's assistant that 'I come here and see no-one at Staff headquarters and so I tell him that an English General Officer expects ... some recognition especially as they left me and mine to defend Belgrade.'[15] In response he gets an apologetic call from the COS himself, a carriage and an orderly.

Troubridge's latent misogyny, already observed in his behaviour towards Una, surfaces in his attitude to the Serbian wives and the many female nurses and doctors who have come out to Serbia in a private capacity to assist the wounded and injured. Referring to the wives of the Serbian General Staff officers he notes, '... the women have decided they won't walk at all and wherever they go they must be taken in automobiles and railways. Here we all stay, which is one more illustration of the extraordinary influence of women in the Semi-East.'[16] He also comments that 'this place is full of women, doctors and nurses and members of various English and Scottish hospitals, who are all quarrelling among themselves as to whether they should go or stay. Most of them come to Phillips for advice but few pay any attention to it, unless it fits in with their own private wishes.'[17] However he is outraged on their behalf at their treatment by the Serbs: 'one can never forgive Serbia for their treatment of the hundreds of English women who came out and nursed their army ... they have left them to go [on the retreat through Albania] on foot enduring the greatest privation ... while their own women have been transported in luxury.'[18] The Victorian in him does not think that women should be there at all, but is outraged that they are treated unchivalrously when they are.

Troubridge compares the Serbs to a small tribe no bigger than the population of north London and mocks the Serbian elite's pretensions to being European, writing, 'We see clearly that most of this country is humbug,' and 'They think they are wonderful and there is nothing left for any man to desire in their country.' He later adds, 'truly an unattractive people when nothing more can be got out of people and they come out in their true colours which are ugly enough.'[19] Ernest's notes perhaps suggest someone struggling to understand the culture of a war in a remote land and his frustrations at the limited attention in either London or among the Serbian authorities his mission attracts.

That he was capable of being two-faced in his opinions can be seen in his later writings. In 1918 Ernest provided the foreword to a book of lectures on the Serbs by the Reverend RGD Laffan. In it he writes, *inter alia*:

> I have lived among the Serbians during the past three years, in days, and under circumstances, which encourage the revelation of every human attribute: in the days immediately following their first success, when they triumphantly flung out of Serbia the 'Punitive expedition' of their powerful neighbour and relentless enemy: in long and weary days of tenacious defence: in the days of overwhelming and treacherous attack upon them, with hope of succour growing less and less: in days of terrible marches in a fighting retreat through their beloved country under moral and physical conditions surely never paralleled in the history of any nation: in the days of regeneration of all that was left of them: and finally in days of eager and reckless fighting to regain that which they had lost. The qualities which they have displayed throughout these fateful years should especially appeal to the inhabitants of our Empire. A love of freedom and country as deeply implanted as our own. A loyalty to friends that does not falter under the greatest temptation, and a chivalry so innate that hundreds of our countrywomen could walk hundreds of miles through a great army in a harassed retreat, through a fleeing peasantry in a disorganized and strange land, and yet fear no evil.[20]

His private notes surely reflect his real feelings regarding this 'truly unattractive people'. Nonetheless, the Serbs appreciated his efforts, particularly in the defence of Belgrade and in helping organise the retreat to the Albanian coast. By order of the Crown Prince

Troubridge was awarded the 'Order of the White Eagle First Class' (of which the Prince was Grand Master) in January 1916 and the King gave him the 'George Star with Swords, 3rd and 4th class'.

Neither did his one-time correspondent forget him for, on his return to the UK he was received by King George V with the Queen and Princess Mary also present on 8 February, a singular honour in those protocol obsessed times.

In his journal Ernest noted the dates of letters he wrote to Una and those he received from her, although regrettably he did not record the contents of them. At the start of his ordeal, she was clearly on his mind. He commented that she 'must be anxious concerning the fate of the "Troubridge Hospital",'[21] – the British Naval Hospital doctors and nurses put together by Una earlier in the year. On 1 December he received a letter from her dated 11 November. He wrote to her on 10 December and again on the 14th, and on the 24th Lieutenant Hilton Young, fresh from the UK, reported that he had seen Una but brought no communication. On New Year's Day 1916 Troubridge wrote to his wife again and on 12 January he received three letters from her – but all written in October – on the 9th, 13th and 15th. He wrote again on 15 January.

By 27 January, now in Rome and making his way home, he confided to his journal that he had had no reply to the telegrams he had sent her from both Taranto and Rome, days earlier. Finally he received both a wire and a letter (dated 20 January) on the 29th. And on 30 January he wired Una that he would be starting for home that day on the 11 p.m. train (after dinner at the Embassy).

Troubridge had written regularly (five times) during the period and sent three telegrams. Una had sent no letter since the one dated 11 November (but three letters before then) until her eventual response of 20 January. And she replied only once to his three telegrams. For three months she had ignored him. Because on 29 November she and John had become lovers and Troubridge was now a cuckold.

# 17

## Back Home; Religion, Rejection and Salonika 1916–1918

Returning home, Ernest had not seen Una for nine months; he had arranged (through his telegrams from Rome) for her to meet him at the railway station, but at the last minute she feigned illness and stayed away, living in a hotel room. He had to sleep at his club. Ernest found Una 'unresponsive'.[1] She had been generally and openly consorting with John for some time now and it was seen as a scandal among those who cared about such things. Ernest's reputation, still regarded with suspicion, was not enhanced by this open defection and immorality. He found it a social humiliation that 'inspired him with rage, called for revenge and barred him from London life'.[2] He was on half pay and his wife did not wish to see him, not even on the occasion of his daughter Mary's wedding, when he attended alone. Eventually they met and Una told him that she would remain his wife in name only and that she was being treated for 'neurasthenia and a venereal infection'.[3]

For some time she had believed that Ernest had infected her with syphilis, and told friends that he should never have married, knowing he had it, and that he had condemned her to years of suffering. In fact there is no evidence to suggest that this was true, but Ernest resented the implication deeply and it hurt him to hear it said. His son Thomas tried to intervene with Una, visiting her to urge her to return to Troubridge and suggesting that there would be a great scandal if she carried on as she was. But Una sent him packing with the retort that she could reveal something that would be even worse than cowardice (presumably, the claimed syphilis).

In June Ernest was promoted to Vice-Admiral; but this should not be seen as a sudden change of opinion within the Admiralty and an endorsement of his actions. Such promotion was automatic upon seniority – one out, one in – and he could take little solace from it. He was not offered any post to go with the promotion and remained unemployed, brooding on the state of his marriage and his sullied reputation.

## Religion

Ernest was received into the Roman Catholic Church in 1916. In so doing he was, in several ways, moving in a counter-cultural direction. He had grown up with the Gurneys, Quakers one and all. Indeed the Gurneys had been central to establishing a particular brand of Quakerism, Gurneyism, (which today represents the views of around 49% of Quakers world-wide). Following the teaching of John Joseph Gurney, brother to old Daniel, they aligned themselves with protestant teaching and favoured working with other protestant churches. The navy, Ernest's 'family' for nearly 40 years, was strongly Church of England. Divine service was held on deck each Sunday and followed the Anglican rite (although when in port, other denominations were often allowed to go on shore and seek out their own churches). Catholicism was still suspect and anti-English. Catholics had been debarred from voting and holding public office until the Catholic Emancipation Act of 1829 and Catholic dioceses were only introduced, to great public outcry, in 1850; to join the Roman Catholic Church was still, to many in the elite, to put oneself at odds with polite society. And to admit to profound religious belief at all was against the *Zeitgeist* of the age.

The first half of Victoria's reign had seen a revival in religious belief and practice following the Georgian 'age of reason'. The massive swing in population density away from villages and into cities, and the desire of the ruling classes to keep the proletariat 'in their place' through the opiate of religion, led to a massive church-building boom (5,550 new Anglican churches alone in the mid-part of the nineteenth century) and a significant rise in religious belief and attendance. By the 1851 census over 50% of the population claimed to have attended church; but this was its apogee. As Matthew Arnold reflected in his 1867 poem *Dover Beach*, the 'melancholy, long withdrawing roar' of the 'sea of faith' showed religion in retreat. By 1901 church attendance had fallen to 30%. And although the absolute numbers remained the same (as the population had almost doubled over the same period) religious belief was waning. Only 9% of the population regularly attended church on a Sunday and a third of these were Catholic. On Easter Day 1901, the key festival in the Christian calendar, only 1.9 million people went to divine service – just 4% of the nation.

Myth and magic was under attack from science and empiricism. Logic, not revelation, was coming to the fore. And growing prosperity, at least for some, rendered the belief in a much better afterlife less compelling. Darwin and Huxley's promulgation of the doctrine of natural selection had established itself in the public mind such that even some prelates were seeking to deny the literal truth of the Old Testament (such as Charles Gore, Bishop of Worcester, Birmingham and eventually Oxford). And philosophy and science were wreaking havoc with the intellectual basis of religion. In 1903 two seminal works were published: Moore's *Principia Ethica* and Russell's *Principles of Mathematics*. Together they represented the storming by science of the Bastille of received religion. George Moore's work established a new basis for morality and the con-ception of the 'Good'; he saw the contemplation of beauty, love, truth, the pleasures of human intercourse and the enjoyment of beautiful objects as key elements of the Good. It was the philosophy of aestheticism, the pursuit of pleasure and the freedom from orig-inal sin. Bertrand Russell's work was, on the other hand, the apotheosis of logic. And as such he demonstrated, *inter alia*, that the existence of a deity or an afterlife was, at best, only a conjecture.

Further he argued that religion was positively harmful, intellectually, morally, socially.

The loss of belief in revealed scripture and the advance of science led to the promulgation of quasi-scientific, quasi-religions. The growth of spiritualism in the early part of the twentieth century will be considered in Chapter 19. Another such aberration was theosophy, actively promoted by Madame Blavatsky, whose followers included the poet W.B. Yeats. Theosophists sought to understand the mysteries of the universe and the bonds that unite the universe, humanity and the divine, exploring the origin of divinity and humanity, and of the world. They thus tried to discover a coherent description of the purpose and origin of the universe – and failed.

During the 1850s the word 'secularism', coined by the radical George Holyoake, began to enter the lexicon and in the 1860s it was followed by T.H. Huxley's neologism 'agnostic'. Secular societies began to spring up along the length of Britain, in an almost lineal descent from Chartism. And, of course, atheism and humanism found their voices. George Bernard Shaw was a strident atheist; Ezra Pound and T.S. Eliot, to name but two, were vocal in their humanist beliefs. Marx, who saw religion of the opium of the people and a means of class control, supported atheism and saw it as an ally in the class struggle.

Alongside the erosion of religious belief came significant advances in technology. Into Ernest's world came massive weapons of destruction (the *Dreadnought*, the torpedo, the 15-inch gun). In 1904 another Ernest, Rutherford, wrote *Radioactivity* and in 1910 he demonstrated the existence of the atom. The motor car began to appear on our roads (the Motor Car Act of 1903 required registration and licensing, the Ford model T was first made in 1908). Railways and electric tramways were at their peak. New drugs were being synthesised (such as aspirin in 1897). There seemed no limit to what science could achieve. And against this background Ernest, a career sailor, a man for whom violence and destruction were the tools of his trade, became a practising Roman Catholic. He moved the other way. In the new age of reason he became a proselyte and a man who ignored science for a deeper revelation. Why?

A first and obvious answer is that Una had converted to the Roman church before him and his own conversion might have been to curry favour with her and prevent a divorce, as Catholics were doctrinally forbidden to dissolve the bonds of marriage. This would be a Machiavellian stratagem and would imply no commitment to his new faith. But in fact he continued in the faith for the rest of his life. Or it might have been for aesthetic reasons. Many people were attracted to the Roman rite for its elaborate garb, ornate churches, ritualistic and opulent services. Indeed this was at the very heart of both the Camden and Tractarian movements of the mid-nineteenth century and which led to John Henry Newman 'crossing over' to the Catholic faith. And, of course, life in the navy was founded on ritual, pomp and routine – piping on board, ritual dress codes, raising and lowering of flags, deference to seniority – all acts which have a reflection in the arcane enactments of the Roman rite.

Una herself, in a letter to the *Catholic Herald* written in December 1942, said in explanation that 'perhaps the crossed keys which he always wore on a ring that had belonged to his Great-Grandfather exerted a beneficial influence'. Or perhaps not.

Faith can give structure and meaning to existence. Ernest, with his marriage on the rocks and his career ruined, might have felt the need for an emotional prop to give meaning back to his life, a sanctuary where he could escape from the realities of his world (and perhaps the war). Did his experiences in the retreat from Serbia cause him to look away from science to a deeper meaning behind the horror and tragedy? And belief in a deity takes away responsibility for one's own actions and satisfies a hunger for absolution; manifest destiny takes charge; decisions can be avoided.

In his Serbian journal Troubridge records that he went to church with Colonel George Phillips, the British Military attaché, on Sunday 21 November 1915. They attended the Roman Catholic cathedral in Mitrovitza. Was this an informed choice? It was probably not for Phillip's sake – his alma mater was Uppingham School which has a protestant tradition of worship. Was Ernest already on a journey of faith?

In the end, it is speculation; but I believe that Ernest was seeking certainty. His career on the back burner, his reputation tarnished, his wife distanced and unhappy, he sought the conviction, non-judgemental forgiveness and warmth of organised religion. He needed support.

21 June saw Ernest attend a requiem mass at Westminster Cathedral, conducted by Cardinal Bourne in remembrance of the men lost at the battle of Jutland on 31 May and also the slightly later loss to a mine of HMS *Hampshire* with War Minister Field Marshall Kitchener on board. This must have been a poignant moment for Troubridge, for three of the four ships he had commanded in the 1st Cruiser Squadron were sunk at Jutland and the dead included many men who had served with him. (6,784 British sailors were lost at Jutland and three battle cruisers and three armoured cruisers sunk. Nonetheless it was a tactical victory for the British Grand Fleet under Jellicoe. HMS *Hampshire* sank on 5 June, carrying Kitchener to Russia on War Office business with the loss of 578 men.)

Likewise the unpleasant memories of his trek across the mountains into Albania must have been unwillingly recalled to Ernest's memory on 28 June as he attended a service at St Paul's Cathedral, part of a Britain-wide campaign to celebrate Serbia's national day. The Archbishop of Canterbury preached the sermon, in which he expressed the nation's deepest sympathy for her ally in her distress and offered an assurance that Britain would stand with her to the end. Apart from Troubridge, the great and the good of the allied nations' War and Foreign Offices attended, together with the Serbian Relief Fund and representatives of the nursing detachments serving in Serbia. Three hundred refugee boys sang the Serbian national hymn under Christopher Wren's great dome, a tune Ernest had not heard since the horrors of the great retreat through the mountains.

Serbia was, phoenix-like, *riviviso*. The Serbian army was being reformed in Salonika to fight on the Macedonian front. And for

Ernest, it must have come as a relief from the rounds of memorial services and the disintegration of his marriage when, in September, the Imperial Serbian Crown Prince, Aleksander, asked for Troubridge to be assigned to his personal staff as an advisor and aide. So it was, on the morning of 14 September, that he returned to the Balkans, accompanied once again by Henry Fitch as his secretary.

The lifestyle was less than demanding. They acquired two Stude-baker cars which they used to go shooting with 12-bores. Ernest felt the exercise involved kept him fit and he loved to shoot on the Vardar marshes where they bagged copious amounts of widgeon, teal, snipe and even lesser bustard. When not shooting Troubridge had a small Serbian naval corps of officers and men to command and he set them building boats albeit without the proper materials or tools. Meanwhile Fitch played hockey for the army and the navy and in the summer played cricket and went on bathing picnics with the doctors and nurses.

But the Crown Prince was anxious to do more and at a round table conference in May 1917 it was decided to send Ernest to London to voice the needs of the Serbian front. Subsequently, at a War Cabinet meeting of 21 May 1917 it was stated that Ernest had telegraphed the Admiralty, stating that the Crown Prince had expressed the desire that Troubridge return to England to appraise the British government of the situation of the Serbian army which, in the Prince's opinion, would probably collapse soon (this was accompanied by a plea for 30,000 additional troops and 12 siege guns for action on the Salonika front). Ernest was duly recalled and he sailed aboard the destroyer *Arnot* for London.

He had assumed he would stay with Una, but she booked him a room at the Charing Cross Hotel instead and refused to see him until she and John could meet with him and tell him formally of their relationship, and that they were going to set up house together in Datchet, near Windsor, which would allow Una to be free of Troubridge for good. He was appalled. It was a social and personal humiliation. He had disliked Una having interests of her own any-way. Now she was in a lesbian relationship and spent all of her time with John communicating with her dead cousin (see Chapter 19), who had in turn been John's lover. Ernest thought she had gone insane.

In August Una and John went to Datchet, farming their daughter Andrea, a constant inconvenience to Una, out to a dog-breeder in the town and in September Ernest returned to the Balkans, via Greece.

## Salonika

The attitude of general distrust and reserve that the Admiralty showed towards Troubridge throughout his time in the Balkans is typified by a War Cabinet minute of 12 September 1917. This notes that Ernest had been appointed to the personal staff of the Prince Regent and *in no way* represented the Admiralty (author's emphasis). Troubridge continued to be *persona non grata* as far as the powers-that-be were concerned. The minute went on to record that General Corkran had been appointed by the Chief of the Imperial Staff to the Serbian HQ as liaison and that the question of recalling Ernest should only be discussed once Corkran had taken up his post and if he reported that Ernest's presence was causing him difficulties.

The reformed Serbian army, under the direct command of Prince Aleksander, mustered at Salonika where British and French military forces were also based; and here they languished, seeing little action and dying of a variety of malarial and other diseases (in 1917 over 20,000 British troops were laid up with malaria, and in the three years of the campaign malaria accounted for ten times as many men entering hospital as did wounds on the battlefield; 34,762 men were invalided home as unfit for duty as a result of the disease, the equivalent of two infantry divisions).

The overall theatre commander, French General Sarrail, was a particular *bête noir* for Troubridge and the War Cabinet. In March 1917 Troubridge had written, through his ADC, to Prime Minister

Lloyd George personally complaining that there was a lack of vision and no workable war staff under Sarrail who, as a 'political' appointment was not up to the mark. The only energy came – according to Ernest – from the Serbs. And a Cabinet minute of 10 September complains about Sarrail's lack of activity.

Occasional attempts to push out of the peninsula were made and life was nowhere near as cushy as, *inter alia*, French Prime Minister Clemenceau made out with his jibe that they were the 'Gardeners of Salonika', but life followed a generally leisurely pattern. On St George's Day 1917, for example, the British cruiser HMS *St George* held an 'at home'. Ernest and the Crown Prince attended, the Royal Serbian Band provided the musical entertainment, the great and the good of Salonika and their families were served with Her Majesty's finest food and drink, and the captain of the cruiser was awarded the Order of the White Eagle 4th class with swords. And on 23 March 1918 the British made an amphitheatre outside Salonika to hold the final of the British army boxing championships in front of 16,000 men, British commanding general Milne attending and invited as guest of honour.

Ernest's Victorian *pater familias* attitude towards Una had already been noted. During 1917 an incident occurred which demonstrated that he was a product of his times in other ways too – in his chivalric view of womankind. The British general in charge in the region issued an order that officers were not to give lifts to nurses in their cars. Ernest was apparently furious and said the navy would never obey such an order. Such discourtesy, Fitch later wrote, was 'entirely foreign to his nature where ladies were concerned'. He ordered Fitch to pick up two nurses at his earliest convenience and drive them to the CinC's army house. When Fitch was later stopped by the very same general, having in his car a pair of nursing ladies, a huge row developed which was settled only by Ernest giving Fitch a dressing down for obeying his orders – and then putting his arm round him and telling him to forget it; it was for form only.

At last, the relaxed existence changed in June 1918 when the French General Franchet d'Esperey was appointed to command all

Allied Forces in the region. His opening address to his subordinates set a new tone; '*Je attends de vous une energie farouche*' (I expect from you a savage vigour).[4]

Suddenly there was great activity as the autocratic, severe and self-willed d'Esperey decided on action against Bulgaria, in the face of opposition from his superiors at home whom he disdainfully disregarded. His polyglot army of French, Serb, Italian and Greek soldiers began to stir for a final reckoning. Aleksander was delighted at this new turn of events (the more so as d'Esperey was apparently impressed by his attitude and ambition) and he and Ernest became deeply involved in the Frenchman's staff group where the urbane and imposing (and French-speaking) Troubridge made a favourable impression.

Ernest played two parts in the revival of the Serbian army and the smooth running of the Crown Prince's suite. As a naval officer he created the nucleus of a navy arranging for the training of about forty men, who had mostly been boatmen on the Danube, through cruises in British warships. They wore British uniform, except for the cap-ribbon, and officers dressed in soldier's khaki. Their only craft, the *Greater Serbia*, was an old Greek torpedo-boat (the ex *Beta*, built in the 1880s and sold to a private company in 1912) that had since been used as a ferry and was bought by the Serbian government in Corfu. Although unarmed, the little steamer with the Serbian ensign at the stern did useful work at Salonica in towing men and stores from place to place on the shores of the Gulf. More importantly it did much to lift the Serbian morale as a very visible signal of regeneration.

As a diplomat, Ernest took a more important role. With some knowledge of international relations from his time as Chief of the Naval War Staff, and aided by Commander Alfred Stead RNVR, his Chief of Staff and a Balkan expert (author of *The truth about Bulgaria* and *Servia by the Servians* and son of W.T. Stead the journalist and quondam editor of the *Pall Mall Gazette*, who died in the *Titanic* disaster), Troubridge worked hard to keep Allied relations with the Serbians at the right point of amiability and confidence. When puzzled by Allied rulings or pronouncements, the Serbs came to him for explanation and reassurance. When they had some views which they wished to put before the Allies they submitted them to Ernest first. His role became that of an unofficial ambassador and the confidence that the Crown Prince placed in him allowed him to smooth the path for Franchet d'Esperey and his staff.

The Allies attacked on 14 September, the Serbs and French most heavily involved, and by the end of September it was all over. Weakened by food shortages and resenting the Germans in their midst, the Bulgarian army signed a formal armistice on the 30th and laid down its arms.

D'Esperey now advanced onto the Danube and appointed his British sailor friend as Admiral Commanding on the waterway. Troubridge had only a small naval force to support him, 55 men, six petty officers and a Captain C.V. Usborne in command. He requested further support from the Admiralty, a full naval brigade and mines; instead he received some gunboats and a strong rebuke for accepting the appointment from a foreign general (a criticism that might in part have been driven by the divergent agendas at play; the British wanted to go to Constantinople and protect the routes to India, d'Esperey wanted to go to the Danube and drive on into Germany through the 'back door'). The navy also still harboured its resentment of Ernest for his 'betrayal' of naval tradition in 1914 and Their Lordships attempted to prevent him taking command of the British riverine forces, but d'Esperey took no notice – he had chosen his man.

On 5 November d'Esperey set off for Belgrade and that night dined with The Crown Prince at the Serbian General Headquarters, Troubridge in attendance. However, Ernest's desire to prove himself in battle was disappointed for the Austrians surrendered before he reached the Danube and no action was necessary on the rivers.

Finally, the war all over the world ended on 11 November. Weary soldiers and sailors from many countries and in many far flung lands began the long trek home. The war to end all wars had itself ended. 62.5% of Serbian males between the ages of 15 and 55 had perished in the conflict and the country had been laid waste. Ernest returned to England.

That Ernest's service to Prince Alexander and the Serbian people was appreciated by the Serbian Royal Family can be seen in the haul of medals and honours that he and his service attracted. He was made a Grand Officer of the Order of Karageorge (with swords), an award in the gift of the King in, in 1918, for 'services to the Royal Family' and held by only four other worthies. This was coupled with being made a Grand Commander of the White Eagle (with swords) in April of that year. The Italians appointed him a Knight Grand Cross of St Maurice and St Lazarus, an order originally founded by the House of Savoy in the sixteenth century, also in 1918.

The French presented him with the Croix de Guerre avec Palme in the October, no doubt as a reward for the Bulgarian campaign and at d'Esperey's urging. Not to be outdone the Greeks weighed in making Troubridge a Grand Officer of the Order of the Redeemer at the beginning of 1919 and the Romanians followed in May, appointing him Grand Commander of the Order of the Star of Romania. Finally the newly formed Kingdom of the Serbs, Croats and Slovenes, under the Kingship of his friend the former Crown Prince of Serbia, gave him their version of the Croix de Guerre in October.

This impressive medal haul gives weight to Ernest's abilities as a diplomat and tactful aide during his time at Prince Alexander's side and of the impression made on the supremely irritable and mon-archist Franchet d'Esperey (who, incidentally, received the Serbian honorary army rank of 'Voivoda' in 1921 in recognition for his role in liberating the Balkans, and had a boulevard named after him in Belgrade). And it's odd that the man who could use his skills in this way had little ability to do so with his colleagues and wife.

# 18

## *Wray, Separation and back to the Danube, 1917–1921*

Away from the Balkans, Troubridge's seniority took him to the rank of full Admiral in January 1919 (on the retirement of Admiral Bernard Currey). In the King's birthday honours list of 3 June of the same year he was made a KCMG – Knight Commander of the Order of St Michael and St George. This should not be seen as implying any weakening in the Admiralty's views regarding Ernest. The Order was in the personal gift of the King and was given specially to honour individuals who have rendered important services in relation to Commonwealth or foreign nations. The citation recognised his 'valuable service as Admiral Commanding on the Danube'.[1]

While Ernest had been hobnobbing with foreign royalty and generals in the Balkans, Wray had been assessing his position. After the *Goeben* (and Hamilton's damning assessment that he should never command at sea again) he had been placed on half pay with the stench of cowardice never far from his reputation. He made repeated attempts to see first Churchill and then other members of the Board of Admiralty to put his side of the story but was rebuffed. However, there was a shortage of experienced captains and he was finally given a command. In February 1915 he was appointed to command the second-class protected cruiser HMS *Talbot*. She was an obsolete *Ellipse* class vessel mounting a mixed armament of 6-inch and 4.7-inch guns and had in fact been present at the Battle of Chemulpo Bay, witnessed by Ernest in 1904. Launched in 1895 she had been pulled out of reserve at the outbreak of war and in March 1915 was sent under Wray to the Dardanelles to act as a gunship in the shelling of the defending forts, part of Churchill's ill-fated campaign to force the strait by sea power alone and leading directly to the carnage of Gallipoli. Using Wray freed up a captain of better standing for sea duty.

Wray performed well at the task and covered the evacuation of Anzac beach in December, partly recovering his reputation and gaining the award of Companion of the Distinguished Service Order (DSO) in March 1916 as a result. The citation read 'In command of HMS *Talbot* which was the mainstay of the supporting cruisers and light craft at Sulva from 6th to 10th August.'[2] Clearly Wray had shown some backbone on this occasion.

In 1917 he decided to write to Jackie Fisher, under a sworn affidavit (dated 3 August), to put his case. Fisher was, of course, no longer in power and Wray wrote to him at an address in Studland Bay, Dorset. In the declaration he accuses Troubridge of lying at his court martial.

Wray began by stating that as a consequence of the result of the court of inquiry and court martial his personal honour and character as an officer had been impugned by allegations of cowardice and default and that he had repeatedly been denied the opportunity to clear his name. With a view to clearing his reputation he wanted to put the record straight. Wray then went on to detail the events of the 6 and 7 August and recapped the evidence that he gave at the court martial. He added that he was denied the opportunity to be present at the court of inquiry and was refused permission to make a statement to clear his honour at the court martial. He noted that, in Ernest's evidence, it was his – Wray's – opinion that led to Troubridge abandoning the chase and that this led others to blame him for the escape and stain his reputation. Churchill, he noted, stated that 'poor Troubridge was wrangled by his Flag-captain for two hours eventually was persuaded by him not to fight'.[3]

In his version of the night's events he explained that he had initially enthusiastically supported Ernest's plan to cross *Goeben*'s 'T' and all but wrote out the signals to that effect for him. On reflection he began to doubt the wisdom of the plan and returned to Troubridge to inform him that perhaps the plan should be reconsidered. He stressed that at no time did he advise him to abandon the chase – and was astounded when Ernest did just that, initially thinking that the squadron had hauled off to gain time while he asked the CinC for instructions and to reconsider the problem.

Then Wray dropped his bombshell; he stated that Troubridge gave evidence at the court of inquiry and in his report to Milne that Wray had told him the guns of his squadron had a wide spread and that they were not effective above 8,000 yards; and that he had seen the *Goeben's* shooting and it made a perfect pattern at 15,000 yards. 'These statements and assertions I absolutely deny,' he went on, 'and did so in letters that I wrote to the Admiralty [in 1915] ... I did not make any such statements to the Rear Admiral nor did I make any reference to the spreads of the guns or their effective range.'[4] In other words, Troubridge was a liar, trying to save his skin at Wray's expense.

Wray closed by saying that Milne's conduct was approved officially by the Admiralty and Troubridge was cleared with honour, but that he had received no reply to his request to be exonerated and that 'I have been under great anxiety of mind which is detrimental to my best service to my country and I beg that the above statements be taken into consideration with a view to clearing my honour and my reputation.'[5]

It is a remarkable document – a man, considering himself traduced, accusing his then superior of lying at a naval court. But why send it to Fisher? He was definitely not flavour of the month at that time and had no formal powers, other than being chairman of the government's Board for Innovation and Research. For whatever reason and through whatever route, the paper reached the Admiralty, for it now resides in the Admiralty papers at Kew. And nothing was ever done about it.

As for Wray, he commanded *Talbot* until January 1916 and was then unemployed again for two more years. Finally, at the beginning of 1918, he took command of HMS *Caesar*, launched in 1896 and now obsolete and useless, capable of only 9 knots and being used as a depot ship in the Med and later the Aegean. It was not a prestigious post and he held it for less than a year. A promising career had turned to dust and he was placed on the retired list in 1922 having had no further employment, and maintaining his resentment of Ernest to the end.

Wray and Henry Horniman met in the Hyde Park Hotel years after the *Goeben* incident. In his autobiography Horniman records that he asked Wray if he had ever given Troubridge advice to call off the chase. 'No, he said, it was an absolute lie.'

## Separation

In January 1919 Ernest made an unannounced visit to Una at the Datchet property. There was, according to her diary, 'an unpleasant scene'.[6] Una refused to see him unless John was present. Una and John reaffirmed that they were lovers and that John had bought a large house (Datchet was rented) for them to live in as if they were a married couple. An enraged Troubridge accused John of having wrecked his marriage and threatened legal action, a position he retreated from on sober reflection. Instead, at John's suggestion, her lawyer drew up a 'deed of separation'. Such a deed was the only legal way for Catholics to part and took the form of a financial settlement together with arrangements for children and property. To ensure that he signed, Una provided the solicitor with supposed medical evidence that Ernest had infected her with syphilis.

Ernest had no option and signed on 8 February, in the certain knowledge that an even more public scandal would result if Una sued for a judicial separation. As part of the arrangement, Troubridge re-made his will and specifically stated that under no circumstances should Andrea be left under the guardianship of John should he and Una both die (he specified Laura Hope as one potential guardian). But then he had second thoughts. On Una's birthday, 8 March, Ernest's solicitor wrote to Una seeking custody of Andrea. Back the ladies went to Sir George Lewis, His advice was uncompromising – this was a subterfuge and the original deed was binding. Ernest gave up.

There was one last sordid chapter to this sorry tale of marital break-up. On 30 May Ernest received his 'K' to his CMG. He was now Sir Ernest Troubridge and his wife Lady Troubridge. Una seized on the title, despite the separation, and used it for the rest of her life, putting it on her visiting cards and writing paper. Such a title had value. She never saw Troubridge again.

Separation was but one cross for Ernest to bear. The story of the escape of the *Goeben* remained in the public eye throughout the war and even after the end of the war. *The Times* too up the offensive in its 22 January 1918 edition: 'The story of their escape from Messina represents one of the greatest of our blunders, it is also the first of a long series of unfortunate episodes about which the public have been told that no one was to blame, while the suppression of the facts has prevented any opportunity of forming an independent judgment. A blunder, a pail of whitewash, and rigid secrecy – these are the three main factors in the *Goeben* case.' The same newspaper then followed this up immediately after the Armistice on 15 and 22 November, asserting that 'the escape of the *Goeben* was the critical event which directly led to the Ottomans joining the war on the side of Germany'. For the Ottomans, the *Goeben* was 'a pledge and proof of Germany's power'. The Ottoman public 'believed she was invincible'. The writer went on to add, 'no two warships have had such an important effect upon the war as the *Goeben* and the *Breslau*. They will always be remembered in naval history' and 'very rarely in war has a single error had more far-reaching consequences'.

Milne's and Troubridge's tactics were ~~widely~~ also widely criticised. Souchon, writing after the war, stated, 'The English should have waited before the Straits of Messina and nowhere else, but so confident were they that the *Goeben* and *Breslau* must try and break through to the Adriatic in order to reach an Austrian port that they thought it safe to wait in the Straits of Otranto.' Jackie Fisher, no doubt regretting the idleness of his beloved battle cruisers on that fateful day, wrote to *The Times* on 9 September 1919 asserting 'the British Navy should have been able to sink the *Goeben* before she reached the Dardanelles. The *Goeben* escaped because the British battle-cruisers that were in the Mediterranean were not used.'

The Admiralty's reticence to reveal the full details of Ernest's court martial and why Milne had not had to face a court of inquiry had started with Churchill's declaration in November 1914 that information relating to the escape of the *Goeben* could not be released without prejudice to vital interests and continued well after the war. On 12 March 1919 Harold Smith, the Conservative MP for Warrington, asked the First Lord of the Admiralty 'whether he will lay upon the Table of the House the Report of the proceedings of the Court of Inquiry which inquired into the cir-cumstances attending the escape of the *Goeben* and the *Breslau*, and which acquitted Admiral Sir Berkeley Milne of all responsibility therefor?'.[7]

The response which came from the Financial Secretary to the Admiralty, Dr Thomas MacNamara was: 'As stated in reply to a question by my hon. Friend the Member for Portsmouth North on the 26th February, no Court of Inquiry was held in the case of Admiral Sir Berkeley Milne. The Admiralty issued a statement on the 30th August, 1914, to the effect that: "The conduct and dispositions of Admiral Sir Berkeley Milne in regard to the German vessels *Goeben* and *Breslau* have been the subject of the careful examination of the Board of Admiralty, with the result that their Lordships have approved the measures taken by him in all respects".'[8]

With his next question, Smith then hit the nail on the head. 'Is the Right Hon. Gentleman aware that there is a certain amount of anxiety lest officials in the Admiralty are maintaining secrecy in order to shield themselves or other officials, and though probably that is untrue, does it not point to the necessity of the Admiralty issuing whatever reports there are of inquiries or courts-martial held on the subject?' MacNamara batted him away.[9]

But the Admiralty's ordeal was not yet over for on 27 March Commander Carylon Bellairs took up the attack: '... asked whether he [the Prime Minister] is now in a position to announce a decision as to the publication of the proceedings of the Troubridge court-martial, and the dispatches in regard to the escape of the *Goeben* and the bombardments of the forts in the Dardanelles?'[10]

Again the luckless MacNamara had to stonewall the bowling; 'I have been asked to reply to this question. It is hoped that it will be possible to announce the decision next week.'[11]

No decision was announced. Ernest saw himself to be a man whose personal Calvary seemed unending.

## Back to the Danube

Ernest's children had long fled the nest. Thomas Hope had followed him into the navy and served at sea during the war. He was now pursuing a naval career that would see him achieve the rank of vice-admiral in the second global conflict. His daughters had married; his wife had deserted him for a lesbian lover; his naval career and reputation were sullied. There was nothing to keep him in England.

In the aftermath of war there were many tasks of rebuilding to be undertaken by victors and losers alike. One such was the reopening of the mighty Danube for commerce. The Danube was a critical trade artery for many European and Balkan states and its management and control had always been a bone of contention. The Commissions of the Danube River were authorised by the Treaty of Paris (1856) after the close of the Crimean War. The most successful was the European Commission of the Danube (in French, *Commission Européen du Danube*), the CED, which had authority over the three mouths of the river – the Chilia in the north, the Sulina in the middle and the St George in the south. The CED had originally been designed to last for only two years. Instead, it lasted for eighty-two. A separate commission, the International Danube Commission, or IDC, was authorised to control commerce and improvements upriver beyond the Danube delta and was supposed to be permanent, but it was not formally organised until after 1918 and only then in a different guise.

The Allies urgently needed a Balkan specialist to head the newly revived committee. One who would represent the victor's interests and be acceptable to the Serbs, Romanians and other interested non-European parties. The choice fell on Troubridge and he swiftly accepted; for him it was another chance to rebuild his reputation and position – and get away from the gossip. For the Admiralty it got a potential troublemaker out of the way. And so, on 20 February 1919, Ernest returned to the Balkans and set up his office in the ex-Austrian Embassy in Belgrade.

This new body, named the Inter-Allied Danube Commission (IADC), was convened under Troubridge's leadership and comprised additionally American, French and Italian representatives. Later in the year non-enemy states were admitted in equality with the great powers; the group met with some success in reopening the river, despite the difficulties. However, Troubridge's tenure was short, for by the end of the year he was replaced by a Foreign Office nominee, without protest from the Admiralty. He returned to the UK and this at least allowed him to attend Buckingham Palace on 18 December to receive his KCMG from the King in person.

While away in Eastern Europe he had once again incurred the Admiralty's enmity (and that of the Foreign Office) by interfering in the life of the short-lived (March to August 1919) Hungarian Soviet Republic formed by the revolutionary Béla Kun. The genesis of the problem was the antipathy between Hungary and Romania, the latter having entered the war on the Russian side in an attempt to gain territory in Hungarian Transylvania. At the end of the war there was much territorial jostling at the borders of Hungary and Romania and the Paris Peace Conference recommended the establishment of a neutral zone between the two countries, a border which definitely favoured Romanian territorial ambitions.

Hungary was not officially informed of this proposal until one Lieutenant Colonel Vix, a French officer, informed the President of

Hungary on 20 March, describing the line as a 'temporary political frontier'. He turned it into an ultimatum by demanding a response within 32 hours. The information sparked predictable nationalistic anger which eventually led to the fall of the government and control being taken up by an ex-muck-raking journalist and quondam aide to Lenin, the communist agitator Béla Kun. Kun sought Bolshevik support and soldiers, formed a Red Hungarian Army of his own and prepared to fight the Romanians for the disputed lands.

It was against this background that Troubridge received the news that Lt-Col. Vix had been taken hostage by the Communists along with the crew of a British motor launch (ML *228*) which had been with Vix to provide secure communications. Ernest had orders not to interfere with the situation in Budapest, but the opportunity to make the headlines and add some lustre to his faded career proved irresistible. He hurriedly put together a small scratch force consisting of a British motor launch under the command of Captain Haggard, and the former KuK (Austrian) monitors *Bosna* and *Enns* flying the British and French flags respectively, which left Baja on 22 March for Budapest.

It was a shambles. Vix was not a hostage but the crew were, apparently willingly for they were flying the Red Flag on their craft, under Communist control. Over the next four days Haggard successfully brokered the release of the crew of ML *228* and the return of the vessel, only to find the Reds had seized another motor launch, ML *210* and carted off the crew. More negotiations were required to secure their freedom. At the same time Haggard had to organise the breakout of his monitors whose largely Croat crews were getting edgy at the sight of machine guns and artillery being deployed on the river banks.

Finally getting away safely Haggard reached Baja on 27 March – the same day that Vix left Budapest, peacefully and safely, by train. Ernest was in trouble. British naval vessels had been captured, their crews imprisoned or turned. This could be another Court of Inquiry. By dint of suppressing Haggard's report and glossing as best he could his own communique to the Admiralty, he got away with a reprimand for not following orders. It seems that when it came to following orders, Ernest just couldn't get it right!

Concurrent with the demise of Béla Kun's short lived revolution was the so-called 'Battle of Baja' of June 1919, when two monitors and four armed gunboats of the former Austrian navy, now under the control of revolutionary Hungarian forces, were seen to approach the British Danube base of Baja. A Lieutenant Watney, commanding the motor launch ML *236*, sallied out to attack them and defend the base only to discover that they were coming to surrender. For his courage and subsequent tact in negotiating their submission he was awarded the Distinguished Service Cross on 17 October of the same year, only to die a week later. Troubridge endorsed his DSC award with the comment that he was 'a most efficient officer. He behaved with much gallantry on the 26th June, 1919, when his vessel being stationed at the advanced look-out position above Baja, on the Danube, he proceeded to the attack of the approaching Hungarian Flotilla ... when he subsequently found they had come to surrender he shewed [*sic*] much initiative and good sense in dealing with the situation.'

Troubridge's involvement with the revolution in Hungary did not end there. The Romanians finally invaded in July and crushed the Red forces, demanding that power be handed over to the Social Democrat Party. To ensure that the Romanian encroachments be controlled and that food and supplies could continue to flow, Troubridge needed to ensure he had full control of the riverine communications. He occupied the dockyard and railway sidings to deny them to the Romanians and to prevent their destruction. As he had a flotilla of launches and their crew under his command, he retained more leverage over the military situation than any other Allied actor in the theatre. He refused a Romanian demand to hand over control of the Danube, limited Romanian military operations across the river, and assisted in the distribution of food aid by river which was impossible on land.

Food was a preoccupation for Troubridge, both in the eating and the provision of it. He boasted that he had got food through to starving Serbia in November 1918 and to starving Budapest in November 1919.[12] On 9 December 1920 in a speech given in Vienna as head of the IADC, he noted that 'a generous and far-sighted economic policy by all states must ensure that the products of the earth and the results of man's industry are not withheld from the teeming millions to whom they are a vital necessity whatever their nationality.'[13] This, as he saw it, was his primary mission in keeping the Danube open for commerce and safe for shipping.

Ernest's position also led him to be a frequent dinner guest. For example, the American General H.H. Brandholtz, sent to Budapest as part of the Inter-Allied Military Commission to supervise the disengagement of Romanian troops from Hungary (arriving 10 August 1919), entertained him to dinner on 18 August, 31 August (together with Commander Stead), and 28th September (with Ernest's son Thomas and Lt-General Tom Bridges, a one-legged war hero), and was invited in his turn to dinner with Trou-bridge and the Romanian Chief of Staff, Vasilescu on 22 September. Brandholtz confided to his diary that 'our chef is steadily improving and turned out a meal that would have done credit to Paris'. Meanwhile, among this prandial excess, Ernest had warned on 22 September that there was only five days' food left in the city due to Romanian seizures and the mining of the river by Béla Kun's associates. Nonetheless his small flotilla was able to keep the Danube clear of interference and allow food shipments to reach the city despite the depredations of the Romanians. The mines remained a problem. By early November 40 out of 60 had been neutralised but at the cost of 24 minesweeping sailors' lives.

Troubridge also took a stance politically in the affairs of Hungary. After the communists under Béla Kun had seized power a counter-revolutionary government had been formed by the forces of the right, which asked Admiral Horthy (considered by Hungarians to be a war hero) to take command of its forces. However, before he could act, and as noted above, Romanian, Czechoslovakian and Yugoslavian forces invaded Hungary and later the Romanian army overthrew Kun's government. When the Romanians evacuated

Budapest on 14 November 1919, Horthy entered the capital at the head of the national army. A gala performance was organised at the Opera House for the 16th to celebrate Horthy's symbolic liberation of the city.

Troubridge and his suite attended this performance, much against the wishes of the Foreign Office and their representative on the ground, Sir George Clerk, who did not want to be seen to be legitimising an unelected and royalist-leaning government – opposition that was in vain after all, for in 1920 Horthy was declared Regent and Head of State, a position he held until his deposition in October 1944.

Troubridge knew and respected Horthy (and corresponded with him after his return to England) and had lent his support to him. It is interesting to speculate why he did so, thereby implicitly giving the British government's support to Horthy's position. First, Horthy was a naval officer; their shared profession must have allowed a bond to form. Second, Ernest's main concern was to keep the Danube open and foodstuffs flowing; if a 'strong man' in government could further this goal then all well and good. Third, the ruling elite of Hungary were of the Catholic faith (although Horthy wasn't) as were the counter-revolutionaries who had appointed Horthy to his leadership role; Ernest was too and had monarchist values and ties of his own.

His stand on behalf of Horthy bought him much kudos in Hungary, but little with his own government. Lord Hardinge, Permanent Under-Secretary for Foreign Affairs at the Foreign Office, said of him, 'There is no doubt that Troubridge has throughout acted most injudiciously.'

All of this involvement in Hungarian affairs made him somewhat of a cult hero to the Hungarian population. When he appeared in his box at the opera, the audience applauded. When the Magyar Foreign Minister, Lovaszy, was told by the Romanians (with an army of 40,000 at their backs) that he must immediately sign a separate peace and alliance, Lovasky came to Ernest who immediately sent a strong note to the Romanian HQ. Nothing further was heard of separate treaties. When Romania attempted to bring about further anarchy in Hungary by releasing Bolsheviks back into the country (in the hope that the Paris Peace Conference would mandate them to stay to fight communism), Troubridge countered by starting a passenger service up and down the Danube to allow those likely to be infected by disaffection the chance to go to see family separated by the war and distance and buy cheaper food. He was to all intents the dictator of Hungary, although always giving precedence to Admiral Horthy.

Because of, or in spite of, these actions, Troubridge was removed from the IADC before the year's end. However, the FO's representative did not work out and a further suggestion favoured by the Admiralty was turned down; there was nothing for it – with studied reluctance, the Admiralty asked Ernest to return to the East; and so in February 1920 he turned over his naval responsibilities on the Danube to a Commander Leith and set off once more for Belgrade. Here in the Balkans, where the populace neither knew nor cared of the stigma of his court martial or the scandalous behaviour of his wife, he could live out the fantasy of the life he thought he should have. As his flag-ship he acquired a steam yacht, the SS *Alexander.* And as his flag-lieutenant he appointed his son, Tommy.

No doubt his tact and presence were helpful in corralling the differing opinions round the table. The conference reconvened in Paris in September 1920 to draw up a definitive statute for the river. Austria, Belgium, Bulgaria, the Kingdom of Serbs, Croats and Slovenes (later Yugoslavia from 1929) – a new formation to be ruled from 1921 by Ernest's bosom pal Aleksander the quondam Crown Prince of Serbia – France, Germany, Great Britain, Greece, Hungary, Italy, Romania, and Czechoslovakia were represented. It took six months, but on 23 July 1921 the basic convention was signed. The European Commission of the Danube was re-established, and all the old treaties and regulations were confirmed. Ernest had done well.

The Foreign Office certainly thought so for on 7 April 1921 the Secretary of State (Lord Curzon, the same peer who had embarrassed Churchill into sending Ernest to Serbia through his question in the House of Lords), through his PPS, wrote and told him so. The letter asserted that 'the measure of success attained in circumstances of no small difficulty appears to be largely attributable to the judgement and firmness which, as President of the Commission ... you have displayed in reconciling the conflicting claims of the riparian states ...'[14] Finally someone in authority approved of his actions!

However, Ernest's escape from court martial still rankled in the Admiralty. In a small-minded gesture he was put on half pay in June 1920, officially because he was being remunerated by the Foreign Office (actually by the Danube commission through an account in the FO) for his service on the IADC, and in July of the following year he was placed on the retired list. He had accepted that it was now a certainty that, short of war again, he would never hold a naval command at sea. His naval record shows that he retired 'at his own request'. Perhaps this was a recognition by Ernest that the events of 6/7 August 1914 were never truly going to leave him free of taint. His pension would be more than his half pay anyway. Better to get on with life where he was appreciated – among the Serbs and other Eastern Europeans.

We can get a picture of Troubridge during his time with the IADC from the descriptions of him left by some who worked with or around him. Paymaster Commander Edgar Burrows, who was to become treasurer to the Commission, described Ernest as 'a charming courtly old gentleman who pats you on the back and calls you "my boy".'[15] The same writer left an account of Troubridge's management style which accidentally casts further light on his relationship with the Admiralty. In 1920 the Admiralty had allocated Troubridge £5,000 to get food moving on the Danube; the money was regularly promised but not forthcoming and eventually, in exasperation, Ernest ordered Burrows to make the difficult journey back to London to collect it. After many vicissitudes and by dint of going to Paris and the Supreme Economic Council (to whom the IADC was subordinate), Burrows obtained the money and returned (with more difficulties) to the Balkans. Troubridge greeted him with, 'Hello my boy, have you got it?' After Burrows had answered in the affirmative, Troubridge simply said, 'Good boy!'[16]

The American journalist Harry Frantz wrote a rather hagiographic article on Troubridge in 1920. In it he states that Ernest's 'affable and democratic personality fascinates all who meet him ... the Admiral is rather old and grey.'[17] Clearly, Ernest retained the charm and affability that had distinguished him in his younger days. But it is interesting that both writers describe him as 'old'. He was in fact only 58 in 1920; time was perhaps not treating him well.

But in the Balkans Ernest had found a mission and gained some respect. He had the satisfaction of knowing that the population were grateful for his efforts. He was lauded and lorded in a position of power. He rubbed shoulders with rulers and high ranking officers. His opinion was sought. Here, at least, he was appreciated; but not so at home.

In the aftermath of the Great War, the South African Millionaire Sir Abe Bailey commissioned a set of three paintings to feature the British statesmen, military and naval commanders of the conflict. In 1921 Sir Arthur Stockdale Cope, under this commission, painted 'Naval Officers of World War One' (now at the National Portrait Gallery) which depicted twenty-two admirals in the Admiralty Board Room. Beatty, Keyes and Tyrwhitt take centre stage, their stars having risen in the later stages of the war. Near the back are the three fallen admirals, Cradock (at Coronel), Hood and Arbuthnot (both at Jutland). Battenberg, who had not served since 1914, was depicted. Madden, Burney, Browning, Napier, Leveson who had all done very little during the war, were included. Troubridge was not.

# 19

## Scandal, Court and Churchill, 1919–1924

After the death of Mabel Batten in 1916 – which had allowed a troublesome threesome to become a committed couple – Una and John became increasingly interested in spiritualism and psychic research. They took to attending séances with a medium, Mrs Gladys Osbourne Leonard, and came to believe that Batten's spirit was with them. John, still desperate for 'Ladye's' goodwill and affection, despite causing her pain by transferring her attentions to Una, was particularly obsessed by these sessions and they became a daily occurrence. Una kept copious notes of the revelations and happenings that occurred and the two of them would write these up as a journal.

Spiritualism and psychic research, séances and the occult were fashionable interests and pastimes in the late nineteenth and early twentieth centuries. The great leap forward in scientific under-standing that took place in the nineteenth century and the advent of such 'magic' as telephones and radio lent credence to the thought that there might be an 'electromagnetic world' that we did not yet understand. Additionally, the Victorians were preoccupied with death, and scientific advance gave rise to the thought that this final frontier too could be conquered or at least better understood. Mediums held séances at which tables moved, apparitions appeared and messages were received; credulous, grieving or just sensation-seeking attendees took these as signs of the existence of a spirit world.

Interest in the phenomenon grew during and after the First World War as the massive slaughter caused the bereaved to seek ways of recontacting their lost ones. As but one example, the writer and member of the elite intellectual group 'The Souls', Pamela Tennant, mistress and later wife to Foreign Secretary Sir Edward Grey, turned to spiritualism on the death of her son 'Bim' and his close friend Raymond Asquith, son of the Prime Minister, on the Somme in 1916. The Victorian 'fairy painting' movement, made famous by such as John Anster Fitzgerald, Joseph Noel Paton and Richard Dadd was a cultural expression of the craze, as was the penchant for 'ghost story' books from a wide range of authors from Mrs Gaskell to Edgar Allen Poe. Sir Arthur Conan Doyle was a noted believer and great publicist for the movement. His writings did much to proselytise such beliefs and he wrote a two-volume history of the movement. The first Labour Member of Parliament, Keir Hardy, was another well-known adept, as was W.T. Stead, crusading editor of the *Pall Mall Gazette*, who was fascinated by 'automatic writing' which he hoped would enable him to have contact with the 'other side' and in particular his deceased son. At the time that Una and John became adepts the movement was at its peak.

There was even a quasi-scientific body to further the investigation of spiritualism, the Society for Psychical Research (SPR), founded in 1882. In 1917 a former president of the society (and also a member of the Royal Society, a far more rigorous and august body), Sir Oliver Lodge – a physicist involved in several key developments in wireless telegraphy and who too was a follower of Mrs Leonard – encouraged Una and John to write a research paper based on their experiences for consideration by the SPR. This paper, entitled 'On a series of sittings with Mrs Osbourne Leonard' was presented to the Society on 31 January 1918, John herself reading it aloud. It ran to 200 pages and she presented only the first half.

Another distinguished member of the SPR was St George Lane Fox-Pitt, son of the explorer and founder of the Pitt-Rivers Museum in Oxford, Lieutenant General Augustus Henry Lane Fox. Fox-Pitt was a scientist, a pioneer of the electric incandescent lamp and an inventor whose interests also encompassed moral education and psychical research. In character he was said to be independent, strong willed, generous and rash. All of these traits would shortly come into focus. At the end of the reading he stormed out of the room, partly in disgust at the quality of the report but largely because he disapproved of John and her overt behaviour. Nonetheless, Lodge was delighted with the reading and a second presentation of the paper was arranged for 22 March. Additionally, it was mooted that John should be nominated for election to the council of the SPR.

But, while the spirit world might be proving auspicious, the real one was not. Cara, Mabel's daughter, who nursed a deep resentment for John on account of her taking her mother's affections away from her and their open lesbian relationship, complained to the secretary of the SPR in June, saying that the report was all a pack of lies. When informed of this, John threatened legal action and the danger to her psychic success temporarily abated. And there the matter lay until January of 1920.

Like most of his peers Fox-Pitt was a member of several London clubs, one of which – The Travellers – he shared with Ernest. Una's defection and her open relationship with John was the talk of clubland and Fox-Pitt might well have felt some form of outrage given his interest in moral education. It was widely stated, from the comfortable embrace of a deep armchair and a brandy and soda, that John was a lesbian, a seducer of wives and addicted to 'sorcery'.

With whatever motivation, Fox-Pitt provided a sympathetic ear for Troubridge. He told Ernest of the SPR paper and Troubridge told Fox-Pitt how John had 'wrecked his life' and seduced his wife.

John's election to the council was slated for January and Fox-Pitt, in a fit of moral outrage, determined to prevent it. He wrote to Isabel Newton, the secretary, stating that 'Miss Radclyffe Hall is a grossly immoral woman'. He continued 'Admiral E. Troubridge has recently been home on leave and has, in my presence, made very serious accusations against her. He said that she had wrecked his home. She ought not to be co-opted as a member of the council ... my own feelings about her have been confirmed by what Sir E. Troubridge told me.'[1] In a separate letter he made the same points to the editor of the Society's newspaper and said that he would do everything in his power to prevent John's election. 'Immoral' was a powerful word to use in those times and both his correspondents asked him if it was not a dangerous accusation to make. Fox-Pitt responded, 'Admiral Troubridge *is not afraid of anything* [author's italics] and would be quite willing to make this statement publicly. He would not mind it at all coming out.'[2]

John was informed and immediately demanded a retraction. When Fox-Pitt refused, she went to the lawyer Sir George Lewis and took out a slander action. John had money to use the law as a weapon and Lewis was the perfect man to wield it. He was one of the most prominent lawyers of his time and had handled many high profile cases, including acting for Charles Parnell and the Irish Party. Knighted by Gladstone, he was a friend and confidant of Oscar Wilde and refused to act for the Marquis of Queensbury out of friendship in the fateful trial which destroyed Wilde's position and reputation. He acted for Edward, when Prince of Wales, in shielding him from his many indiscretions. His obituary described him as 'not so much a lawyer, more a shrewd private enquiry agent' and he was an expert at libel cases. John had pulled out a big gun; but Fox-Pitt stuck to his case and the trial went ahead before the Lord Chief Justice, Rufus Daniel Isaacs, and a 'special jury' (a jury of one's peers, wealthy, titled etc., rather than the general 'great unwashed').

The case was a shambles. Fox-Pitt conducted his own defence and Ernest, when subpoenaed by Lewis, wrote to deny that he had ever made such allegations about John. It appeared that, after all, the Admiral was afraid of 'anything'. Seeing that he was on a sticky wicket, Fox-Pitt tried to defend that he used the word 'immoral' to describe the paper presented to the SPR rather than the author of it.

The jury, hampered in their deliberations by the fact that lesbianism was not contrary to any statute law, eventually found against Fox-Pitt and John was awarded £500 in damages. Fox-Pitt appealed and a retrial was scheduled but it never took place and the case faded away.

The damage had, however, been done. The press had thoroughly enjoyed the case (the *Daily Mail* had headlined its coverage of the first day of the trial 'Spirits in Slander Suit' and published a large photo of Ernest on its front page) with its spiritualism, psychics and the whiff of sexual deviation. Reports of the trial were carried all over the Empire, including the Adelaide *Advertiser* and the *Ashburton Guardian* of New Zealand. The country in general now knew that John was a practising lesbian, as was Una. Ernest Troubridge had been publicly embarrassed and, in the face of danger, had shown that he was at best unwilling to enter a public argument and at worst, gun-shy. The gossip behind his back grew louder.

## Churchill

In 1923 Winston Churchill published the first of four volumes of his 'magnum opus', *The World Crisis*. Initially seen as a history, it quickly became recognised as in reality a glorification of the role played by Churchill in the eventual victory.

The *Dundee Advertiser* (a more important newspaper then than now, as it was at the centre of the D.C. Thompson empire – and Churchill had been MP for Dundee between 1908 and 1922) captured the mood of Churchill's decriers in its review of the book, commenting:

> Mr Churchill is a very great egotist and in placing himself on the cosmic stage his egotism attains to an amusing quality ... the reader has exhibited to him the titanic events of the war happening around and in no small way controlled by Mr Churchill. We see him teaching the great sailors at the Admiralty, which perhaps was to be expected. But we also see him offering guidance to the Foreign office, to the Minister of War and the Commanders in the field. He has a policy for everybody ... Mr Churchill's narrative is really a determined laying down of the proposition that whoever made mistakes, he made none.[3]

In absolving his Admiralty of blame for the disasters that befell the navy in 1914, Churchill traduced the reputation of brave Kit Cradock, dead Louis Battenberg and the still very much alive Ernest Troubridge. A furious Ernest felt forced to respond, and wrote for private publication 'A Rough Account of the *Goeben* and *Breslau*' in his own defence. It was written longhand in a ledger and for some reason he never came to publish (or finish) it.

In it he stated, 'Mr Churchill has written a book … it is perhaps coloured by a desire to prove his administration is without fault. He cannot understand why "Admiral Troubridge changed his mind" – but I never changed my mind; as I propose to relate a line of conduct relative to the *Goeben* has been laid down *ab initio* and from that I never changed,'[4]

Ernest attributes to the French Admiral Boué de Lapeyrère the quotation 'I do not understand why the British Admiral was blamed for the *Goeben* escaping seeing that his squadron was merely a squadron of observation'[5] and blames the diplomats in Constantinople for not informing him that Souchon would head for Turkey. He reiterated that he believed that he would have battle cruisers in his company and that he had agreed with Milne that without them *Goeben* was a 'superior force'.

A self-serving tone creeps in towards the end of his self-justification: 'I believe it is better for the Navy that officers be prepared to suffer rather than bring a "cause celebre" … which [would] split the officers of the Navy for many years.' He adds that 'many individuals and newspapers offered to take my case up. I refused them all.'[6] The martyr clings to his cross.

In ending his account of the affair he concluded, 'It was necessary that someone should suffer for the escape of the *Goeben*. The First Lord of the Admiralty certainly was not going to accept responsibility for any blame. The First Sea Lord, Prince Louis of Battenberg, neither … the CinC was not prepared to shoulder any responsibility. There only remained myself.'[7] It seems that both Churchill and Troubridge were intent on re-writing history.

# 20

## *Endings, 1924–1926*

Ernest continued in post at the IADC until 31 March 1924. The Foreign Office expressed appreciation of his services in a note of February in the same year. The Admiralty said nothing.

In 1924, the year of the British Empire Exhibition and the Paris Olympics, there was nothing in England to keep Ernest there. His children were married and long since not close to him. His ex-wife and her relationship with John – becoming ever more public and embarrassing as both women's respective fame increased – was a source of irritation and scandal. They were openly living together and consorting with a group of lesbians drawn from the artistic and theatrical world. Una had adopted a distinctive garb of bobbed hair and a monocle, seen at the time as an 'advertisement' of her lesbianism. The painter Romaine Brooks, herself a lesbian, painted Una in that year portraying her in a tailored man's suit and a monocle, holding two dachshunds by the collar.

Troubridge's reputation, which he had hoped to rebuild in the Balkans, still carried with it the scent of the *Goeben* despite his success with the IADC negotiations. Milne had published a book defending his own actions and placing the blame on Ernest which, while not a best seller, was no doubt a cause of anger.

The UK itself was in a mess, struggling to come to terms with post-war economic recession and changed societal expectations. The 'land fit for heroes' ('What is our task? To make Britain a fit country for heroes to live in,' said David Lloyd George, during a speech at Wolverhampton, 23 November 1918) was turning into a hollow joke.

The General Strike was only two years away, there had been coal and railway strikes three years previously and industrial unrest was raising its head everywhere. Unemployment had reached a record 11.3% in 1921 and fearful of inflation government cut back on public spending, reducing work opportunities still further. The advent of Ramsey MacDonald's Labour party led coalition in January 1924 did nothing to stem the downward slide into chaos and despair. As the *Spectator* magazine commented in its 5 April 1924 issue, 'the strike of London tramway and omnibus workers is at an end, after ten days of wholly unnecessary expense and of acute suffering on the part of the public. But we are faced with the possibility of a national lock-out in the Shipbuilding and Engineering Trades, arising out of the strike of the shipyard workers at Southampton; there is a strike of the coal-trimmers at Leith, a building strike at Wembley, and a crisis in the Pottery industry; while over the whole country the terrible menace of another strike in the coal industry broods.'

Troubridge might have been expected to have been politically opposed to Ramsey MacDonald's short-lived Labour government, the first in British history, and probably was. But in one issue at least he sided with it. Both Ernest and the Prime Minister saw that the Versailles agreement, which ended the war and imposed huge reparations on Germany, was bound to fail and lead to further hardship and war. Troubridge blamed the French President, Poincaré (the man who had forced the occupation of the Rhineland) for refusing to consider any alleviation of the penalties imposed.

Ernest was not alone in his view that the Treaty of Versailles, which set out the levels of reparations due from Germany to the Allies and defined the shape of Europe and the future of the ex-Austro-Hungarian possessions in the Balkans and elsewhere, was not fit for purpose. John Maynard Keynes in his book *The Economic Consequences of the Peace* first gave coherence to these views, although many people read it as saying just that they could only lead to a new war. There was also a growing body of opinion that Britain's economic ills were the direct result of the punishments inflicted on Germany and that no good would come from enforcing them.

Troubridge's quondam boss McKenna, Home Secretary after the Admiralty then Chancellor of the Exchequer in 1915–16, now Chairman of the London Joint City and Midland Bank, expressed a different concern. In a speech to the Commercial Club of Chicago in October 1921 he gave his opinion that Germany could never repay her debts. His argument was that in order to earn sufficient money to do so, Germany would have to export massively and the only way to be successful at this was to undercut the competition on price. In his view, this was a direct cause of the two million unemployed in Britain at that time, as German exports were causing great injury to British trade and underselling the UK the world over. He thought the root of the evil of the Versailles treaty was its complete disregard of economic factors.

Ernest clearly agreed with the latter point, for in January of 1921 he had written to McKenna from his vantage point on the Danube. He saw that the 'folly' of the treaty was 'in the carving up of Europe into fragments without regard for the economic life of the popu-lation'[1] and that an Economic Union of the Danube statelets was the only solution. In this he showed unsuspected prescience. Troubridge also focused on the standing armies all these small countries insisted on retaining, each seeking to exploit any weakness in the others' position. 'It should be conveyed to those who owe us money that they must pay it. That they keep up great armed forces, nominally at their own expense, it is actually at our expense which they so indulge and leave their debts unpaid.'[2]

McKenna continued to press his point. He and the chairs of all the other big banks wrote to Prime Minister Lloyd George (whom he loathed) in April 1921 to plead that the settlement of German indemnities be alleviated as the first step towards improved foreign exchange. But the French were adamant and the economic situation got worse.

As for Troubridge, London (he was renting a house in Chelten-ham Terrace SW3) clearly offended him. In July 1924 he wrote that 'London is terribly crowded and almost impossible to get along the streets' and he wanted to be away from the crowds and the innuendo; 'I am really almost homesick for foreign parts.'[3] Against this background, Ernest decided to leave and spend his time in France, whose language he had spoken since childhood.

He chose Biarritz, on the Bay of Biscay in France's Basque region, only 11 miles from the Spanish border. In the eighteenth century doctors had recommended the ocean at Biarritz for its therapeutic properties, inspiring patients to make pilgrimages to the seaside for alleged cures for their illnesses. The town's fame increased when, in 1854, Empress Eugenie (the wife of Napoleon III) built a palace on the beach (now the Hôtel du Palais); and its real cachet came when the British royalty decided to adopt the place. Queen Victoria and Edward VII were frequent visitors and this drew in other crowned heads such as Alfonso XIII of Spain.

To cater for this inrush of aristocratic money, Biarritz's casino opened in August 1901 and the magnificent beaches became famous among the right sort of Europeans and (whisper it softly) even Americans. An English church was established to serve the in-comers, St Andrew's, and the presence nearby of the war cemetery at Du Sabaou no doubt also helped make Brits feel that there was a little of themselves here. The temperate oceanic climate was warm and freezing cold was rare. The sea breezes were pleasant, the milieu likewise. Biarritz became a home from home for a fair sized English community, like its near inland neighbour, Pau.

This was where Ernest chose to set up his residence (Biarritz is, incidentally, the only place where a British Prime Minister has for-mally taken office on foreign soil. On the death of Henry Campbell-Bannerman in April 1908, H.H. Asquith succeeded to the Prime Ministership. Edward VII was on holiday in Biarritz and refused to return to England, citing health grounds, for the official 'kissing of hands'. Asquith was forced to go to France instead in order to formalise his appointment.)

The season was enjoyable. There was dancing and balls, dinners and soirées; not, in fact, unlike the life he had enjoyed on Malta. Ernest's now bulky figure and his urbane, friendly demeanour, coupled with his language skill, made him a popular member of the 'set'. Here he could escape for a while the wearying round of innuendo, newspaper comment and whispered asides.

And it was here, on 28 January 1926, while dancing energetically at a *thé dansant*, that Ernest had a heart attack. He died within minutes. He was 63. The Silver King was no more.

His obituary was published in *The Times* on 30 January. It mentioned a distinguished pre-war career and recapped the *Goeben* affair. In summary, the writer suggested that 'his subsequent employment was not of a kind to afford him much opportunity of distinction. Personally he was well known and highly popular in many countries in Europe.' Damned by faint praise perhaps?

There was to be no large memorial service in the UK. The Admiralty did not mourn his passing. There was no hero's honour service at St Paul's. He was buried in Biarritz, his adopted home, quietly and without fuss, on 1 February. Ex-naval colleagues and friends attended the service, along with his three children by his first marriage. Una and Andrea did not attend.

Back home, on 13 February, the family held a requiem mass for Ernest at J.F. Bentley's magnificent Westminster (Catholic) Cathedral, completed only twenty-three years earlier. The extended Troubridge clan attended and this time so did Una, braving the cold stares and ostracism of the relatives. At the conclusion of the service she left and went straight back to John for comfort and relief.

Ernest's childhood had been with the Gurneys at North Runcton Hall, and Norfolk did not forget him. In All Saint's (Anglican) Church, North Runcton, a memorial was erected by his extended family. Wall mounted, white on grey marble, a rectangular inscription tablet on grey base with a pointed top and containing a coloured shield of the Troubridge arms (for some reason Edith's father's name is wrongly given, as was Ernest's date of entry to the navy). It reads:

IN MEMORY OF
ADMIRAL SIR ERNEST THOMAS TROUBRIDGE K.C.M.G., C.B., M.V.O
3RD SON OF COLONEL SIR THOMAS TROUBRIDGE BARONET C.B.

& HIS WIFE LOUISA. HE WAS BORN JULY 15TH 1862 HAVING
SPENT HIS BOYHOOD IN THIS PARISH, ENTERED THE ROYAL
NAVY IN 1878, SERVING WITH GREAT DISTINCTION FOR
OVER FORTY FIVE YEARS; HIS OUTSTANDING
QUALITIES AS SEAMEN & DIPLOMATIST EARNING
RECOGNITION IN HIS OWN COUNTRY AND IN MANY
LANDS BEYOND THE SEAS. HE DIED AT BIARRITZ
JAN 29TH 1926, AGED 63, & IS BURIED THERE.
ALSO HIS WIFE EDITH MARY, DAUGHTER OF JAMES
DUFFUS ESQRE OF HALIFAX NOVA SCOTIA. SHE DIED JANUARY
10TH 1900 AT ALVERSTOKE & IS BURIED THERE, WITH THEIR
INFANT SON EDGAR GODFREY TROUBRIDGE. HE DIED DECR
28TH 1899 AGED ONE MONTH'

At least somebody cared. Una caused no remembrance to be made.

Ernest's estate at probate was £452. 18s 11d (perhaps £23,000 today). Una learned from the Admiralty that she was entitled to a widow's pension of £225 a year with £25 for Andrea, this despite their long estrangement. At the urging of John's solicitor she petitioned the Admiralty that it should be increased as she was a single woman on her own and supporting a child, ignoring the fact that she and John were living together and she was supported by John's huge fortune. The Admiralty, unknowing, acquiesced to her request.

# 21

## From Beyond the Grave

Even after his death the Silver King continued to trouble the Admiralty. The proceedings of his court martial were never published in his lifetime, or for many years afterwards, and the Admiralty kept its implicit criticism of themselves to themselves.

But in March 1933 the maverick Conservative MP for St Marylebone, Captain Alec Cunningham-Reid – a World War One flying ace who had married (and divorced) a millionairess – asked a question about it in the House of Commons. Hansard records the following exchange:

> Captain CUNNINGHAM-REID asked the First Lord of the Admiralty if he is aware that the proceedings of the court-martial which acquitted the late Admiral Sir Ernest Troubridge, K.C.M.G., C.B., C.V.O., in November, 1914, have never been made public, although repeatedly pressed for in this House; and whether, in fairness to the relatives of this officer, he will now authorise the publication?
>
> Sir B. EYRES MONSELL [First Lord of the Admiralty]: The full proceedings of the court-martial are much too voluminous for publication, and a large part of them is confidential. From the standpoint of the relatives of the late Sir Ernest Troubridge, the following information should, I think, be sufficient. The charge was one of forbearing from through negligence or through other default to pursue the chase of His Imperial German Majesty's Ship *Goeben*, being an enemy then flying. The concluding words of the finding were: 'The Court

therefore finds that the charge against the accused is not proved, and fully and honourably acquits him of the same.'
Captain CUNNINGHAM-REID: Is it not a fact that in the case of the *Royal Oak* the proceedings were published?
Sir B. EYRE MONSELL: I do not know what that has to do with the question.'[1]

The blanket of silence actually continued for much longer – the papers concerning the trial were only made available to general view in 1970 through the persistent efforts of E.W.R. Lumby.

It was perhaps in December of 1939 that the escape of the *Goeben* was finally exposed as the failure of Troubridge's attacking instincts. For at the battle of the River Plate the German 'pocket battleship' *Graf Spee*, named for the destroyer of Cradock's squadron in the same waters 25 years earlier, was hunted down and bottled up in a damaged state by Commodore Henry Harwood and his force of three cruisers. Harwood's force was outgunned, as Troubridge had not been, his adversary possessing six 11-inch guns and eight 6.9-inch with a broadside weight some 1000 pounds heavier than the combined British ships. Bravely fighting and manoeuvring his ships to divide the enemy's fire (just as Troubridge's critics had maintained he could have done), Harwood wounded the beast and forced her into refuge in a non-combatant port. Knowing that he was far from resupply of armament and fuel *Graf Spee*'s captain ordered her to be scuttled and committed suicide.

Both sides suffered casualties, the British losing 73 dead, the Germans 61. One British cruiser, HMS *Exeter*, was severely damaged and had to retire. But the battle fought was the one that most in the Admiralty thought Ernest should have fought in a similar situation, as was the acceptance of the risk to life and *materiel*. First Sea Lord Admiral Sir Dudley Pound wrote to Harwood, 'Even if all our ships had been sunk you would have done the right thing ... your action has reversed the finding of the Troubridge court martial and shows how wrong it was.'[2] Troubridge's assumed cowardice was still a running sore in the navy even after a quarter of a century.

Pound had served under Troubridge as a lieutenant in HMS *Queen*, 1907–1909. Troubridge endorsed Pound's 'report card' in November 1908 'zeal [*sic*] excellent officer, strongly recommend'. On the strength of that, Pound was promoted Commander on *Queen*'s paying off. One wonders what Pound had made of Ernest.

# 22

## *Verdict*

In his response to Churchill's claim in *The World Crisis* that 'Admiral Troubridge changed his mind' (see Chapter 19), Ernest asserted that he never changed his mind about engaging the *Goeben* and at his court martial his defence was primarily that his orders prevented him from giving battle to a 'superior force'. An examination of the signals he sent to Milne and the squadron is therefore instructive in testing the validity of this claim.

On 3 August Ernest signals Milne, 'Do I continue watching the Adriatic?' Milne replies, 'Yes, but *Goeben* is your primary consideration,'[1] A clearer statement of objective is difficult to imagine. Then 4 August sees Ernest worrying about coal for his TBD flotilla. He tells Milne, 'I will do my best to coal destroyers.'[2] Later that day Milne repeats to him the Admiralty order not to get involved with a superior force. They meant, of course, the Austrian fleet should they sally out; *Goeben* has already been stated as his objective and that order had not been qualified in any way.

On 5 August the Admiralty send the general signal 'Commence hostilities against Germany at once.'[3] Troubridge immediately makes his plans and dispositions clear. To his squadron he sends, 'In the event of *Goeben* coming through Messina and entering the Adriatic the squadron will give him battle.' He intends to fight. And to Milne he communicates, 'In case *Goeben* is in these waters I am keeping within 30 miles of Santa Maura. If we encounter her I shall attempt to draw her into narrow waters where we can engage her at our range.' Milne replies that if she comes out at night he should use his destroyers for 'night work' (unlike the Germans the British navy was not trained in night fighting). Troubridge signals Milne, 'I am proceeding to intercept *Goeben* and instructing destroyers to do the same if they have sufficient coal.' He is still intending to give battle. To his ships he sends, 'I have decided to try and cut her off if information proves to be reliable fighting a night action with the aid of the moon', and again, 'The first salvo fired by *Defence* will be the signal to open fire.'[4]

All through 6 August they seek their enemy. As evening falls Ernest signals Kelly in *Dublin*, 'If you cannot attempt anything on *Goeben* during dark hours, shadow her until daylight reporting position and course. I shall be off Fano Island at 4 a.m.' To his squadron he sends, 'I do not propose to engage him in the midst of the straits my instructions being against it [this is not true, he had received no such instruction]. If *Goeben* wishes to fight I shall endeavour to make use of short waters off Fano Island to choose my own range.'[5] Is this the first intimation of a weakening resolve – '*if* Goeben *wishes to fight*' [author's italics]?

The 7th dawns with Troubridge still intending to fight, however. To his ships he signals, 'I am endeavouring to cross the bows of *Goeben* by 0600 (local time 0500 GMT) and intend to engage her if possible ... if we have not cut him off I may retire behind Zante to avoid a long range action.'[6] And yet just over an hour after that signal he communicates to *Dublin* and *Gloucester*, 'I am obliged to give up the chase.'[7]

Obliged by what? By now he had had his fateful conversation with Wray and had suddenly changed his mind. To Milne he signals, 'Being only able to meet *Goeben* outside the range of our guns and inside his I have abandoned the chase with my squadron, request instructions for light cruisers. *Goeben* evidently going to the Eastern Mediterranean, I had hoped to meet her before daylight.' And to his ships he makes the general signal, 'I have decided to abandon the chase.' Four hours later, Milne sends, 'Why did you not cut off *Goeben*, she only going [sic] 17 knots; and important to bring her to action.'[8] Perhaps this is the first sign of Milne getting his own defences in place?

It is clear from these communications that Troubridge *did* change his mind and that it happened around 0330 local time – after he had sat with Wray.

Troubridge's reply to Milne is instructive for it never mentions the argument of 'superior force' on which he was later to rely: 'With visibility at the time I could have been sighted from 20–25 miles away and could never have got nearer unless *Goeben* wished to bring me to action which she could have done under circumstances favourable to her. I could never have brought her to action. ... I would consider it a great imprudence to place the squadron in such a position as to be picked off at leisure and sunk while unable to effectively reply. The decision is not the easiest of the two I am well aware.'[9]

Historians and amateur strategists, war-gamers and naval officers have argued ever since as to whether Troubridge made the correct decision on 7 August 1914 (it was still being set as a Royal Navy staff college question in 1931). Once *Goeben* had changed course and he could no longer hope to pin her to the shallows and coast he knew he would have to fight an open seas engagement. John Kelly and his destroyers had failed in their night-time attempt to disable or otherwise inconvenience the *Goeben*. Troubridge's own destroyers, which could have been very handy to launch torpedo attacks under cover of the cruisers' gunfire, were short of coal and moored up awaiting a collier, although how this was allowed to happen is a moot point

Moreover, he had expected to meet any opposition with at least one battle cruiser in company and this was not the case – and indeed Milne, in strict if stupid adherence to his orders to protect the French transport fleet from the very enemy that Troubridge was thinking of engaging, had taken the battle cruisers off west and was not about to send one back.

So it is easy to suggest that his options were limited and that prudence dictated that he should not attempt to attack his enemy. That might be the case – and the court martial thought it was. But it does not explain his refusal to follow the *Goeben* at a distance, nor take his destroyers and attack – then having them towed back to harbour when out of fuel and acquiescing in the orders that Milne issued to Howard Kelly to turn back (which that gallant and stubborn sailor twice ignored).

A harassing action from behind would have forced Souchon to turn and fight, which would have allowed the battle cruisers time to come up, and Ernest could always have fallen back on them. If he had engaged in a full scale battle what would have happened? The performance of the armoured cruisers under his command on that fateful day when exposed to German heavy shellfire at Jutland in 1916 was poor. *Defence* and *Black Prince* blew up with huge loss of life (and *Warrior* was badly damaged and later foundered) when under fire from German capital ships – ships very similar to *Goeben* in armament and protection (see Appendix 8).

But the example of Harwood in a later war shows what well-handled smaller ships can achieve. Even if Ernest had merely slowed down the *Goeben*, even at loss to his own fleet, it would have been a tactical triumph. *Goeben* was vastly outnumbered in the Med in total and if she could be brought to action she would be overwhelmed.

Troubridge had never been in action – although he had witnessed some of the Russo-Japanese war before hurriedly and inexplicably taking himself out of harm's way. He had never had to wind his courage up to the sticking point. His had been a long and steady climb up the ladder of power and promotion based on his personal charm and clubbable manner. At a point when daring and courage could have turned the tide, he preferred to fall back on the mantras, so engrained in the Vicwardian navy, of following orders and 'father knows best'. He stayed where he was and signalled Milne for orders.

This was a challenge that his classmate at *Britannia*, Kit Cradock, did not fail. At Coronel, vastly outnumbered and badly advised and misled by the Admiralty, he knew that if he could just damage his opponent's heavy ships enough to slow them down or seek port he would have won a significant tactical victory. Of great personal valour himself, he never doubted what he should do, although he knew he had not the means to do it. And so he died in battle. And it was a challenge that Commodore Harwood accepted in 1939 when he and his outgunned cruisers caused the *Graf Spee* to scuttle.

Yet Ernest knew the traditions of the navy better than most. His family had been there at the birth of the Nelsonic legend and the dictum that no captain did wrong who laid his ship next to the enemy; the flag signal 'engage the enemy more closely' was still in the Admiralty signal book. Furthermore, Troubridge must have known that Milne was a poor commander in the field. He had worked with him since 1913 and would have known his personality and weaknesses. It is true that Milne had ordered him to watch the Adriatic for the Austrian fleet. But orders can be wrong – as Fisher said, 'any damn fool can obey orders' – and Troubridge had a wonderful opportunity to damage, slow, and even just follow an enemy that Admiralty orders, though badly written and confused in language by Churchill's verbosity, stressed was the target; although the Admiralty's reluctance to release the transcript of his Court Martial shows that they recognised that some of the blame attached to them.

Troubridge's later war and peacetime career shows no evidence of personal or moral bravery either. His appreciation of the strategic issues facing him on arrival in Serbia was sound and he managed his command in a sensible manner. He suffered, as did many others, in the retreat from Serbia but his input was administrative not martial. His greatest service to the war effort may well have been his refusal to evacuate the Serbian army from San Giovanni de Medua, which spared them from certain destruction. As an advisor to the Crown Prince he used his social skills and physical presence well as a diplomat but took no part in any fighting. He had proved a capable and successful administrator in the evacuation from Albania and did so again on the Danube and as head of the IADC. Indeed he was lionised by the Hungarian people whose national interest he successfully protected from the Romanians and others. But he never had to take instant decisions; he had time to reflect and consult; he was never under the split-second pressure of command at sea in an engagement.

Fisher had said that Milne (and by implication Troubridge) should have been shot for cowardice, like Byng, and there are parallels with Troubridge's case in more than just Fisher's opprobrium. When Admiral Byng failed to challenge the French invasion of Minorca and, taking discretion as the better part of valour, retired to Gibraltar, his 'fellow officers were convinced that the man who had brought such shame and discredit on the service must be a coward'.[10] But in reality Byng was an averagely brave officer of the time and had been a competent captain. However, he lacked the moral courage to face the challenge of ultimate command and was unable to formulate a decision when under pressure and without the guidance of a superior authority

In the Fox-Pitt slander case Ernest retreated from his earlier statements and lied to the court, denying he had ever made them. In his public views regarding the Serbs he, at best, dissembled his real opinions. And Wray had sworn under oath that Troubridge lied at his court martial too. These are not the actions or behaviours of a morally brave man and make it difficult to take anything Troubridge says, especially at his court martial, at face value.

Edith had been the love of his life and after her death he took a much younger wife, possibly flattered by her interest. But in his behaviour towards Una he showed that he was, at heart, an unreconstructed Victorian who expected obedience and indulgence from his wife and family, a trait magnified no doubt by the respect and unquestioning deference that he received as a captain and flag officer. Like Galsworthy's Soames Forsyte, he treated his wife as one of his possessions. Not that Una's character emerges in the best light, given that she was happy to take his money, title and name but gave little in support in return.

Troubridge appears from the pages of history as a somewhat vain and self-obsessed character. He seems to have had few friends in the service. He enjoyed the Serbs because they made him feel important and gloried in the many honours they showered upon him; in public he praised them, but behind their backs he was scathing about them. He enjoyed the adulation of the Hungarians and the position of power and influence that it gave him. But back home he ran away from the consequences of his actions and the scandal, eventually escaping to Biarritz, where he could play the naval somebody, a big fish in a small pool. He went to his grave believing that he had been right not to face down Souchon, admitting no error even to the end. Likewise he saw John, not his own behaviour, as the reason why Una came to take against him and, in time, humiliate him. And his religiosity, his stubborn belief in mystery rather than science, speaks of a man who was capable of believing despite the evidence.

Good commanders at sea must combine the ability to follow rules and processes with the genius to transcend them. The word genius is much abused but here it is used in the Augustinian Latin sense of 'inspiration' or 'talent'. This is surely what Clausewitz meant when he wrote of genius as being 'a highly developed mental aptitude for a particular occupation'; he saw it as being found in those of 'superior intellect whose careers had been shaped by a sophisticated and systematic appreciation of their profession'.[11] Thus possessors of genius gain an 'intuitive understanding of the situation'.[12] This is not dissimilar to Simone de Beauvoir's view that 'one is not born a genius, one becomes one'.

By any account Ernest fails this test. He was not a superior intellect (although he probably believed he was) as Churchill attested and he had not followed a systematic analysis of his profession; the navy's general approach to career development was 'watch Nellie' and once in command the necessary abilities were assumed to descend from heaven and instil themselves in the commander.

The issue of 'instinctiveness' is critical here. Napoleon posited that the calculations required on the battlefield would tax a Newton; but as decisions had to be made immediately only a highly educated instinct could hope to succeed.[13] This instinct seemed wholly lacking in Troubridge. He could follow orders, but he could not shape or rise above them. Undoubtedly, the Admiralty and Churchill contributed to his dilemma, as their constant and continuing attempt at cover up and exculpation suggests, but a real warrior would have cut through such confusion. Remember that his barrister said of him, after the court martial, 'had [Troubridge] been tried for vacillation, no counsel on earth could save him'.[14]

So, was Troubridge a coward or not? It can be argued that it takes some considerable courage to stay constant to a point of view when many others hold the opposite opinion. But that is really stubbornness or arrogance, not bravery. At the end of the day, when the time came to live up to the reputation of his forebears, to the tradition of Nelson and to the siren voice of destiny, Troubridge bottled it. He was not an overly intelligent man. There were many inputs coming in to consider. His flag-captain was whispering in his ear. Unable to formulate a strategy of his own from the silken threads of information that he held, unable to form a clear mental picture of what he might do, with no battle instinct to fall back on, he allowed Wray to be his means of resolving his problem. It was all too difficult; his choice was just to stop and let Milne decide. And if that is cowardice, then Ernest was a coward.

# 23

## *Postscript*

Una and John continued to live together (John's pet name for Una was 'Squiggie'), both becoming famous or infamous for their respective artistic achievements and for their success in breeding prize-winning dachshunds and griffons. Una was recognised as a talented painter and sculptor (the only sculptor of Nijinsky) and a talented translator of literature from French, Italian and Russian (she was Colette's first English translator, Guareschi's for *Don Camillo* and Lazarevski's for *Political Acrobatics* among many others). She befriended many writers, artists and actors and revelled in their company.

John had a long career as an author, writing and publishing many novels, including *The Forge* (1924), *The Unlit Lamp* (1924), *A Saturday Life* (1925) and several volumes of poetry. Her fourth novel, *Adam's Breed* (1926) was a best-seller and won two prestigious literary prizes, the 'Femina Vie Heureuse' and 'James Tait Black'. All of these novels explored covert lesbian themes, but in 1928 she published her magnum opus, *The Well of Loneliness*, regarded by many as the first overtly lesbian novel. The publisher, Jonathan Cape, argued on the bookjacket that 'In England hitherto the subject has not been treated frankly outside the regions of scientific text-books, but that its social consequences qualify a broader and more general treatment is likely to be the opinion of thoughtful and cultured people.'

It caused a furore. The Home Office put pressure on the publisher to withdraw it describing it as 'inherently obscene' and an obscenity trial resulted after which the Chief Magistrate, Sir Charles Biron, ordered that all copies be destroyed, and that literary merit presented no grounds for defence. The publisher agreed to withdraw the novel and proofs intended for a publisher in France were seized in October 1928. Nonetheless, although banned in Britain it was freely available in France and the USA, and by 1943 when John died had sold over 100,000 copies worldwide in fourteen languages. In 1946 Una asked the then Home Secretary, J. Chuter Ede, for permission to publish a memorial edition of *The Well of Loneliness*. Ede, a Labour politician, trade union leader and a teacher, refused, stating that publishing the book could invite court proceedings.

Both Una and John remained steadfast in their Catholic faith. Plaques attached to the pews in Corpus Christi Roman Catholic Church in Maiden Lane, London (then the home church for the Catholic Stage Guild – the actors' church), attest to their regular attendance. Una wrote a biography of John (*The Life and Death of Radclyffe Hall*, eventually published in 1961) and was her faithful consort for nearly thirty years. However the course of love did not run true, for in 1934 John fell for a Russian nurse, Eugenie Souline, and moved her into the ménage, all three women setting up house together in Florence. At the outbreak of the Second World War they left Italy for Devon and in 1943 John died of bowel cancer in London. Shortly before her death John changed her will, leaving everything, including her copyrights, to Una and asking her to make provision for Eugenie, an instruction Una ignored giving only a very small allowance. In a rather macabre veneration, Una had all John's suits altered to fit her and wore them to destruction.

Una Troubridge died in 1963, aged 76. She had instructed that on her coffin should be inscribed 'Una Vincenzo Troubridge, The Friend of Radclyffe Hall'. She wanted to be buried in Highgate Cemetery, where 'Ladye' and John were also interred, but these instructions were not discovered until it was too late and she was laid to rest in the English Cemetery in Rome, where she had passed away.

Laura, Lady Troubridge, born a Gurney and painted in 1880 by G.F. Watts, sister-in-law to Ernest, became a celebrated Mills and

Boon novelist publishing dozens of bodice-rippers and a book on etiquette.

Ernest's son Thomas became an admiral himself and served in both the First and Second World Wars. Naval attaché in Berlin in 1936, he took command of the aircraft carriers *Furious* and *Indomitable* and the battleship *Nelson* before achieving flag rank in 1943 and commanding the invasion of Elba. After the war he was appointed 5th Sea Lord and in 1948, by a quirk of circularity, found himself as Second in Command, Mediterranean Fleet, the very post his father had taken in 1913, based on his father's favourite island of Malta. He died a year later. In 1925 he had married Lily Emily Kleinwort, of Belgian birth, and they raised four children.

Troubridge's two daughters both married but with contrasting fortunes. Mary, whose wedding Una had refused to attend, married Lt-Colonel Robin Otter MC in 1916 while he was serving in the King's Royal Rifle Regiment. They produced four daughters and lived in some style in homes in King's Lynn, Royston and Swinton and Wath, Yorkshire. Otter became a JP in 1936 and was Deputy Lieutenant for the County of Nottinghamshire between 1942 and 1949.

Charlotte (known to the family as 'Chatty') also married in 1916, to Lieutenant Ernest Alfred Collyer Lloyd. Like so many subalterns, whose life expectancy on the Western Front was short (said to be around six weeks), he was killed in action in 1917 while serving with the Scots Guards. In 1920 Charlotte married again, to Daniel Walter Thomas Gurney whose father now owned North Runcton Hall. The Troubridge and Gurney dynasties once more interleaved and Charlotte found security in an old embrace. A courageous soldier (and another member of the 'black button' KRRC), Daniel was awarded the Military Cross for his actions during the advance down the Murmansk railway in 1919, where he was severely wounded.

Andrea, the daughter who was serially farmed out and then sent to boarding schools, was a constant inconvenience to Una and John (one writer noted that she 'seemed to be regarded by [Una and John] as an inconvenient fact whose impact on their life together was to be minimised to the greatest degree possible.'[1] She became an actress (taking minor roles in such deathless classics as 'The Prime Minister' 1941, starring John Gielgud and 'The House in the Woods' 1957) and also worked as a BBC Home Service announcer. In 1933 Andrea married Theodore Nicholson Warren KCIE. He was made bankrupt in 1936. They divorced and in 1948 she married Brigadier Douglas Tulloch Turnbull CBE, DSO, himself divorced and with a brave army record from service with the Chindits. She died in a car crash in 1966.

Berkeley-Milne, as had been noted, did not receive another command and remained on half pay for the rest of the First World War. In 1919 he was placed on the retired list at his own request and in February, without precedent, the Admiralty issued another statement of Milne's absolution from blame for the *Goeben*'s escape to coincide with his stepping down. The full text read:

> On the retirement of Admiral Sir Berkeley Milne, it has been brought to the notice of the Board that this officer's professional reputation is stated to have suffered in the opinion of the public owing to its being generally supposed that he did not take up the Command at the Nore — to which he had been appointed before the War — or receive further employment, in consequence of events connected with the escape of the German ships *Goeben* and *Breslau* in 1914. This is not the case. The Admiralty at the time issued an official statement, which remains on record, exonerating Admiral Milne from blame, and intimating that the general dispositions and measures taken by him were fully approved. It has been solely owing to the exigencies of the Service that the Admiral has not been further employed.

It should be perhaps reiterated that, before the war, Milne had been on extremely good personal terms with the late King Edward and Queen Alexandra and was well known in royal and society circles. Battenberg, who had been instrumental in issuing the first 'absolution', was married to Edward's niece and knew Milne well, as did King George. Having exonerated him once, the Admiralty were clearly unwilling to risk further opprobrium by being seen to have erred.

In 1920 the publication of the 'Official History' once more rattled Milne's cage (see Appendix 9) and he published a book of his own in self-justification in 1921. It was to no avail; he received no further statement of support nor any invitation to play any other role in naval affairs. Always a keen fisherman, deer stalker and a good shot, he devoted time to such pastimes and to his garden at his ancestral residence, Inveresk Gate in Scotland. He died in July 1938, unmarried and with no heir to his father's baronetcy, and bequeathed his collection of rare shrubs and orchids to the Edinburgh Botanical Gardens.

Of Ernest's Balkan naval colleagues, Commander Alfred Stead, Ernest's Chief of Staff in the Salonika campaign, received recognition for his part in October 1919 when he was gazetted with the Order of St Michael and St George for 'valuable services ... on the Salonika front and on *Danube*'. He also received the Order of the Karageorge, Fourth Class, from the Serbians. Captain Bertram Elliot participated in the famous Zeebrugge raid of 1918 and was killed in action there. Lieutenant-Commander Charles Kerr subsequently commanded a naval gun detachment in Flanders and survived the ordeal. Paymaster Fitch, who had served as Ernest's secretary for the entire period 1915–1918, was invalided home from Salonika on Armistice Day with malaria, the complications from which dogged his later life. He took home with him the Order of the White Eagle from the Serbian King and a fiancée, Scottish nurse Elizabeth Lorimer, whom he met while she was working at one of the hospitals. He later became BBC Glasgow Station Director and then Northern Region Director in Manchester

HMS *Bulwark*, a pre-dreadnought battleship built in 1899, was the setting for Ernest's court martial from 5 to 9 November 1914, while she was anchored at Portland. Sixteen days later she was ripped apart by a powerful internal explosion while moored at number 17 buoy in Kethole Reach, four miles west of Sheerness in the estuary of the River Medway. All of her officers were lost, and out of her complement of 750, only 14 sailors survived; 2 of these men subsequently died of their injuries in hospital, and almost all of the remaining survivors were seriously injured. The only men to survive the explosion comparatively unscathed were those who had been in Number 1 mess deck amidships, who were blown out of an open hatch.

Witnesses on the battleship *Implacable*, the next ship in line at the mooring, reported that 'a huge pillar of black cloud belched upwards ... From the depths of this writhing column flames appeared running down to sea level.' Perhaps the most detailed descriptions of the disaster came from witnesses on board battleships *Prince of Wales* and *Agamemnon*, who stated that smoke issued from the stern of the ship prior to the explosion and that the first explosion appeared to take place in an after magazine.

A naval court of inquiry into the causes of the explosion, held on 28 November, established that it had been the practice to store ammunition for *Bulwark*'s 6-inch guns in cross-passageways connecting her total of 11 magazines. It suggested that, contrary to regulations, some two hundred and seventy-five 6-inch shells had been placed close together, most touching each other, and some touching the walls of the magazine, on the morning of the explosion. The most likely cause of the disaster appears to have been overheating of cordite charges stored alongside a boiler room bulkhead, and this was the explanation accepted by the court of inquiry. *Bulwark* died of carelessness, but she took with her the scene of Ernest's acquittal and his shame.

North Runcton Hall, built by the noted architect Anthony Salvin in 1834/5 for the Gurneys and Ernest's childhood home, survived until 1967 when it was demolished to make way for a housing development.

In the village of Burghclere, on the Berkshire/Hampshire border, is a memorial chapel full of paintings based on experiences of the Salonika campaign. Artist Stanley Spencer served as a medical orderly and then a private in the Royal Berkshire Regiment during the campaign. He used his experiences to produce a series of paintings which capture the savage beauty of the Macedonian campaign. They can be seen at the Sandham Memorial Chapel, a memorial to an Army Service Corps officer, Lieutenant Henry Sandham, who died in Salonika, and which was commissioned by his sister to the designs of Lionel Pearson.

Fawcett Wray received no further post after HMS *Caesar* and remained unemployed. He was promoted to Rear Admiral by seniority on 22 May 1922 and was placed on the retired list the following day; in 1927 he reached Vice Admiral under the same rules of seniority. He died while skiing in the Austrian Tyrol five years later, aged 59. A proud, arrogant and clever man, a Beres-fordite and disliked by Fisher, a naval officer from the age of fourteen, his promising career had come to nothing through his complicity with Troubridge's shame.

Aleksander of Yugoslavia, a man who traced his lineage back to the first Serbian uprising of 1804, a member of the Karadjordjevic clan of Serbian rulers, earthy in speech but *soi disant* aristocrat, given to wearing thin-rimmed glasses which, with his sharply chiselled nose, gave him the calculating look of a schemer, ruled Yugoslavia for thirteen years. Originally a constitutional monarch, he reverted to type in 1929 when he seized executive power. In 1934, while on a state visit to Marseille, he was assassinated (along with his French host, foreign minister Louis Barthou) by the terrorist organisations VMRO (the internal Macedonian revolutionary organisation) and the Ustase (the Croatian fascist movement), both of whom opposed him for his denial of their independence ambitions.

Last but not least, Ernest, quondam father figure to the dead King, drifted from the memory of the powers that be, who were no doubt thankful that his shade disturbed them only rarely. The stone over his grave in Biarritz is much eroded now. The inscription has been blurred by the insistent Atlantic winds; but just enough remains to see that there lies an admiral.

# Appendix 1

## *White Feathers*

In August 1914 Admiral Charles Fitzgerald founded the Order of the White Feather with support from the author Mrs Humphrey Ward. The organisation aimed to shame men into enlisting in the British army by persuading women to present them with a white feather if they were not wearing a uniform. They were joined by prominent feminists and suffragettes of the time, such as Emmeline Pankhurst and her daughter Christabel.

The campaign was effective and spread throughout several other nations in the Empire, so much so that it started to cause problems for the government when public servants came under pressure to enlist. Additionally, the campaign was not popular among soldiers who were home on leave as they could find themselves presented with the feathers. Such considerations prompted the Home Secretary, Reginald McKenna, to issue employees in state industries with lapel badges reading 'King and Country' to indicate that they too were serving the war effort. Likewise, the Silver War Badge, given to service personnel who had been honourably discharged due to wounds or sickness, was first issued in September 1916 to prevent veterans from being challenged for not wearing uniform. The writer Compton Mackenzie, then a serving soldier, complained about the activities of the Order of the White Feather. He argued that these 'idiotic young women were using white feathers to get rid of boyfriends of whom they were tired'. The pacifist Fenner Brockway claimed that he received so many white feathers he had enough to make a fan.

# Appendix 2

## *Ernest's Siblings*

Children of Colonel Sir Thomas St Vincent Hope Cochrane Troubridge.
Sons: Thomas Hay (died in infancy), Thomas Herbert, Ernest Charles
Daughters: Laura, Amy Louise, Violet Elizabeth, Helen Cecil

Laura married in 1888 and Violet in 1893. Amy remained unmarried until the late age of 41, marrying in 1917 and Helen remained a spinster all her life

# Appendix 3

## *Laura Gurney's Siblings*

Laura, who married Ernest's brother Thomas and thus became Lady Troubridge, was the daughter of Daniel Gurney's son Charles. Her mother was Alice Maria Princep, daughter of the great art patrons Thorby and Sara Princep of Little Holland House where G.F. Watts lived in peaceful seclusion for the most productive years of his adult life. Her grandmother, Sara Monckton (née Pattle), was the sister of the pioneering British photographer Julia Margaret Cameron and of Maria, who was grandmother to Virginia Woolf.

Thorby Princep's younger son Val, Laura's uncle, became a painter (having been taught by Watts), worked with Dante Gabriel Rossetti, William Morris and Burne-Jones on the Oxford Union decorating scheme and wrote books and plays. Laura had three siblings, Rachel, Thomas and Henry.

In 1866, Charles was declared bankrupt due to the collapse of Overend, Gurney and Co and Alice later opened a millinery shop in London to make ends meet. Rachel worked in the shop and it was there that she was noted by her cousin, Adeline, Duchess of Bedford, who took her into her own household and introduced her to her husband-to-be, William Humble Ward, 2nd Earl of Dudley and an extremely wealthy man.

Rachel married Ward in 1891 and thus became Countess of Dudley. Ward was a close friend of Prince Edward (later King Edward VII) who attended the wedding, as were the Gurneys. He went on to be Lord Lieutenant of Ireland (1902–1905) and (at the urging of Edward, the King) Governor General of Australia (1908–1911). He had an eye for the girls, however, and it was probably as a result of this that a deed of separation was agreed in 1912. Rachel died in 1920, aged 51, drowned through suffering a heart attack while swimming. Ward later married the actress Gertie Miller.

Both Laura and Rachel were considered great beauties, as was their mother, and were painted by G.F. Watts and John Singer Sergeant respectively.

# Appendix 4

## *The Hope–Wilde Connection*

Adrian Hope'was cousin to Constance Lloyd who, in 1884, married Oscar Fingal O'Flahertie Wills Wilde. When in 1895 Wilde was convicted of gross indecency and sentenced to two years hard labour he impressed upon his wife that if she found the management of the children too much for her she should appoint Adrian Hope as their guardian, which she later did.

On his release from prison in 1897, Wilde signed papers turning over custody of his children to his wife and Hope, and undertaking not to attempt to see them. His two sons, Cyril aged twelve, and Vyvyan aged eleven, had lived intermittently with Adrian and Laura at Tite Street (the same street in which the Wildes had set up their home after their marriage) and continued to do so until Constance took them to live in Switzerland, changing her, and her children's, surname to Holland.

# Appendix 5

## *Albania*

Following the Treaty of London of 1912, which ended the first Balkan War, and the Treaty of Bucharest of 1913, which ended the second, the Great Powers imposed on Albania a new King, William Prince of Wied (whose candidature had been pressed by Queen Elizabeth of Romania, his aunt). The Serbians wanted a port with access to the sea. The Austrians wished to deny them this. Albania thus owed its importance and existence to the desire for a buffer state to hold the Adriatic ports between Greek and Austro-Hungarian territory. A strong, Western-facing, Albania was seen as an important barrier to Serbian irredentism by, in particular, the Austro-Hungarian empire; a Germanic king was preferable to them in this regard. His rule, which lasted only from 7 March to 3 September 1914 was doomed from the start.

Immediately following his arrival revolts of Muslims broke out in central Albania against his Chief Minister, Essad Pasha, and against foreign domination. Greece encouraged the formation of the secessionist 'provisional government of North Epirus'. Although an agreement was made to grant extra rights to the Greek minority, the Hellenic army occupied Southern Albania, ostensibly to protect the rights of their fellow Greeks. William's position was also compromised by his own officials, notably Essad Pasha himself, who accepted money from Italy to finance a revolt and to stage a coup against William (Italy having long-standing irredentist yearning of her own in the area). Pasha was arrested on 19 May, tried for treason and sentenced to death but he escaped to exile in Italy.

The outbreak of war bought more problems for William as

Austria–Hungary demanded that he send Albanian soldiers to fight alongside them. He refused, citing the neutrality of Albania in the Treaty of London, and the remuneration that he had been receiving was cut off, rendering him and his treasury, virtually bankrupt.

From around July a state of civil war existed in the country and with the Greeks still in occupation of the south and rebels at each other's throats in the remainder of the country, his regime collapsed. William left the country on 3 September, heading for Venice. Despite leaving Albania he did so insisting that he remained head of state. In his proclamation he informed the people that 'he deemed it necessary to absent himself temporarily'. He returned to Germany and joined the Imperial German Army under the pseudonym 'Count of Kruja'.

Post-war he still retained ambitions that he might be restored, but the Allied Powers at the Paris Peace Conference did not consider it appropriate to restore to the throne someone who had just fought against them. William continued to assert his rights to the throne and claimed to be its king still, but in January 1925 the proclamation of a republic terminated his hopes.

# Appendix 6

## *Verdict of Troubridge's Court Martial*

1.  That on the 2nd August 1914 the Accused left Malta in accordance with the orders of the Commander-in-Chief with the following ships in company: *Defence* (Flag), *Indomitable*, *Indefatigable*, *Duke of Edinburgh*, *Warrior*, *Gloucester* and the 1st and 2nd Divisions of Destroyers, and was informed that 'should we become engaged in war it will be important at first to husband the naval force in the Mediterranean and, in the early stages, to avoid being brought to action against Superior Forces'. He was also informed that *Goeben* must be shadowed by two battle cruisers, approach to Adriatic Coast must be watched by Cruisers and Destroyers. It is believed that Italy will remain neutral but you cannot yet count absolutely on this.

2.  That in compliance with these orders the Accused proceeded towards the approaches to the Adriatic.

3.  That at 3.19 p.m. on 3rd August the *Indomitable* and *Indefatigable* were detached by the Commander-in-Chief and proceeded to search for the *Goeben* west of Sicily.

4.  That on the 4th August the *Black Prince* rejoined the First Cruiser Squadron.

5.  That at 1.45 a.m. on the 5th August the Accused received the Admiralty general signal to commence hostilities at once against Germany.

6.  That on the 5th August at 0.31 p.m. the Accused received news that the Austrian Fleet was cruising outside Pola and at 4.0 p.m. the *Goeben* was at Messina.

7. That at 6.15 p.m. on the 6th August the Accused received news that the *Goeben* had left Messina steering East shadowed by *Gloucester*. That after then *Goeben* and probably *Breslau* were steering N.5p.E. towards the Adriatic. The Accused's action in proposing to arrive at Fano Island at daylight next day was justifiable.

8. That at 11 p.m. on 6th August the Accused was informed by *Gloucester* that *Goeben* was going to the south east. That at that time his position was N.86.E 145 miles from the *Goeben* approximately. That at that time the battle cruisers were disposed as follows: *Inflexible* (Flag) and *Indefatigable* about 30 miles west of Marsala, Sicily, and the *Indomitable* had left Bizerta at 8.0 p.m. after coaling steering eastwards. That the destroyers were at Vasilico Bay, Santa Maura, seriously short of coal and unable therefore to proceed at high speed to attack the *Goeben* at night.

9. That it therefore appeared that the Accused would get no support for the 1st C.S. and that from his then position it was impossible for him to attack the *Goeben* before daylight.

10. That in view of the instructions he received from the Admiralty Accused was justified in considering that he must not abandon his watch on the Adriatic having regard to the transportation of the French troops then taking place between Algeria and France and the possibility of the Austrian Fleet coming out.

11. That in view of the instruction received from the Admiralty by the Commander-in-Chief and repeated by him in his Sailing Orders to the Accused, and also the Signal made on the 4th August, viz – 1st C.S. and *Gloucester* are not to get seriously engaged with superior force – the Court are of the opinion that under the particular circumstances of weather, time and position, the Accused was justified in considering the *Goeben* was a superior force to the 1st C.S. at the time they would have met, viz – 8 a.m. on the 7th August in full daylight on the open sea.

12. That, although it might have been possible to bring the *Goeben* to action off Capa Malea or in the Cervi Channel, the Court

considers that in view of the Accused's orders to keep a close watch on the Adriatic, he was justified in abandoning the chase at the time he did as he had no news or prospect of any force being sent to his assistance.

13. The Court therefore finds that the charge against the Accused is not proved, and fully and honourably acquits him of the same.

# Appendix 7

## *The Family of Thomas Herbert Troubridge and Laura Gurney*

Ernest's brother Thomas and his wife had three children. The eldest, Louise Rachel, married Captain K.G.W. Sherman in 1918 but they were later divorced. She died in 1961 aged 67.

Son Thomas, who became the 5th Baronet, fought in the First World War with the Kings Royal Rifle Regiment and in the Italian theatre where he was awarded the *Croce di Guerre* and Order Crown of Italy for his actions and also received the OBE in 1919. He had additionally served on the general staff. Reaching the rank of Lieutenant-Colonel, he married late, in 1939, at the age of forty-four, to Pamela Clough, but had no children. His mother's literary influence must have been strong for, after the Second World War, he became a writer and art historian (writing books on tactics and *inter alia* 'a guide to the pictures of the Garrick Club'). In 1959 he served as an Examiner of Plays at the Lord Chamberlain's office and died in 1963, aged sixty-eight. On his demise, the baronetcy passed to his cousin, the son of Ernest's son Thomas Hope.

Finally, Rosemary Blanche, born ten years after her siblings in 1905, married Captain R.K. Mackenzie in 1925.

# Appendix 8

## *The 1st Cruiser Squadron After 1914*

The 1st Cruiser Squadron was transferred from the Mediterranean to the Grand Fleet at the beginning of 1915 and came under the command of Rear Admiral Sir Robert Arbuthnot, a man considered by some to have only a limited grip on sanity. Neither the squadron, nor he, were to see the war out.

During the Battle of Jutland on 31 May 1916 the squadron formed the starboard flank of the cruiser screen, ahead of the main body of the Grand Fleet. *Defence* was just to the right of the centre of the line. At 1747 hours *Defence*, and HMS *Warrior*, the leading two ships of the squadron, spotted the German Second Scouting Group and opened fire. Their gunfire fell short and the two ships turned to port in pursuit, cutting in front of the battle cruiser HMS *Lion*, which was forced to swerve out of position to avoid a collision. Arbuthnot had earlier told a friend that he would close to 'paint-scratching' range if he had a chance and when, minutes later, they spotted the disabled German light cruiser SMS *Wiesbaden* he bore down on her, narrowing the range significantly.

A surviving captain of the squadron thought that Arbuthnot might have been concerned that the German ship could fire torpedoes at the British Battle cruiser fleet. Whatever the reason, he seemed to be suffering from tunnel vision for when the two ships reached a range of 5500 yards from *Wiesbaden* he appeared not to notice that they were in range of German heavy units, and they were taken under fire by the battle cruiser SMS *Derfflinger* and four battleships, all less than 8000 yards away. *Defence* was hit by two salvoes which caused the aft 9.2-inch magazine to explode. The resulting fire spread via the ammunition passages to the adjacent 7.5-inch magazines which detonated in turn. The ship exploded and sank with the loss of all 900 men on board.

*Warrior* was heavily damaged by the German gunfire and set on fire in several places. She started to flood, although her engines ran long enough to allow her to withdraw westwards. She was taken in tow by the seaplane tender HMS *Engadine*, who took off her surviving crew of 743, and later abandoned in a rising sea with only four feet of freeboard, where she foundered and sank

*Black Prince* became separated from the British fleet and during the night stumbled upon the German battleship *Rheinland* just before midnight, engaging her briefly and scoring two hits with 6-inch shells. Wandering lost and seemingly unaware of the respective fleet's dispositions, she blundered into the German line of battleships. Despite trying to turn away she was fixed by the searchlights of the German battleship *Thüringen*. Six German ships, including four battleships opened fire on her, with her return fire being ineffective. Hit by at least 12 heavy shells, *Black Prince* sank within 15 minutes with the loss of her entire crew of 850.

*Duke of Edinburgh* survived the encounter and the war but by now the type was recognised as obsolete and she was sold for scrap in 1920.

In 1917 the squadron was re-formed with three of Jackie Fisher's 'large light cruisers' 15-inch gunned, lightly armoured, fast (*Furious* had one 18-inch) and participated in the second battle of Heligoland Bight. They were converted to aircraft carriers later in the war as it was recognised that their lack of armour rendered them very vulnerable to heavy plunging gun-fire.

# Appendix 9

## Milne's Defence

In March 1920 Sir Julian Corbett's magisterial history of naval operations during the First World War was published. *The Official History of the War: Naval Operations, Vol. I* was critical of Milne and his actions during the *Goeben* episode and Milne, who had – it should be remembered – been absolved of blame by the Admiralty in 1914, protested to the Admiralty that he had been traduced and demanded that the book be amended. This the Admiralty declined to do, and so Milne wrote his own version of the events, published by Eveleigh Nash in January 1921.

In a slim volume of rather stiff and outraged prose Milne gives his own version of events; in particular he is at a loss to understand how Corbett can criticise him given that the Admiralty did not! Milne's opening paragraph gives a flavour of the tone and content: 'After the publication in March, 1920, of the *Official History of the War: Naval Operations, Vol. I*, by Sir Julian S. Corbett, I represented to the First Lord of the Admiralty that the book contained serious inaccuracies, and made a formal request that the Admiralty should take action in the matter. As the Admiralty did not think it proper to accede to my request, I have thought it right to publish the following narrative.'

He then proceeds to attempt to rebut the claims of the 'Official History' by presenting his own version of events; much emphasis is placed on how he strictly obeyed the letter of his orders and that the French were able to safely convey their troops, that being the primary (as he saw it) purpose of his mission

At the volume's conclusion, Milne ends in the same pained tones. 'I have accurately narrated the course of events, and the public are now enabled to form a just estimate of the episode. It remains for the authorities to ensure that the *Official History of the War: Naval Operations. Vol. I* is so corrected as to accord with the facts contained in the Admiralty records.'

# Sources and Notes

## Sources

The following institutions have been most helpful in the research for this book; the fact that such huge volumes of information are kept, archived, stored and made generally available to the public is a tribute to our society and to the people who work in, and the trustees of, these wonderful organisations. I thank them for their assistance.

The British Library, London
The Caird Library, National Maritime Museum, Greenwich (NMM)
The National Archives, Kew (NA)
The Liddell-Hart Library, Kings College, London Archives (KCLA)
The Imperial War Museum (IWM)
Churchill Archives Centre, Churchill College, Cambridge (CAC)

I would also like to recognise the value of the following websites:
Wikipedia.com
Dreadnoughtproject.org

## Notes

*Preface*

1. S.R. Dunn, *The Scapegoat; the life and tragedy of a fighting Admiral*, Book Guild, 2014

## SOURCES AND NOTES

### Chapter 1

1. Quoted in R. McLaughlin, *The Escape of the* Goeben, Seeley Service, 1974
2. ibid
3. Troubridge MSS, Caird Library, National Maritime Museum (NMM), Greenwich
4. Quoted in McLaughlin, *The Escape of the* Goeben
5. Quoted in R. Ormrod, *Una Troubridge, the friend of Radclyffe Hall*, Jonathan Cape 1984
6. I am grateful to Mr Chris Potter, secretary of the Old Wellingtonians Society, for digging out the information regarding Troubridge's performance at Wellington and the curriculum at the time

### Chapter 2

1. Quoted in A. Lambert, *Admirals*, Faber and Faber, 2008

### Chapter 3

1. Troubridge naval record, National Archives (NA), Kew
2. Ipse dixit, author's notes
3. Scrapbook, Troubridge MSS, NMM
4. ibid
5. Letter, Troubridge MSS, NMM
6. Quoted in Ormrod, *Una Troubridge, the friend of Radclyffe Hall*
7. Scrapbook, Troubridge MSS, NMM
8. Letter, Troubridge MSS, NMM
9. Troubridge naval record, NA
10. Lady Troubridge, *Memories and Reflections*, Heinemann, 1928

### Chapter 4

1. Admiral Lord Chatfield, *The Navy and Defence*, 2 vols, Heinemann, 1942
2. Quoted in G. Miller, *The Millstone*
3. Troubridge naval record, NA
4. C. Penrose-Fitzgerald, *From Steam to Sail*, E. Arnold, 1922
5. Troubridge naval record, NA
6. ibid
7. Letter, Troubridge MSS, NMM

## Chapter 5

1.  Quoted in K. Rose, *King George V*, Weidenfeld and Nicolson, 1983
2.  Oh, life is a glorious cycle of song,
    A medley of extemporanea;
    And love is a thing that can never go wrong;
    And I am Marie of Romania.

    Dorothy Parker, *Not So Deep as a Well* (1937)
3.  Rose, *King George V*
4.  Letter, Troubridge MSS, NMM
5.  ibid
6.  ibid
7.  ibid
8.  Quoted in M. Waterhouse, *Edwardian Requiem*, Biteback Publishing, 2013

## Chapter 6

1.  Admiral Cresswell, quoted in I. McGibbon, *Blue Water Rationale*, GP Print, NZ
2.  Troubridge naval record, NA
3.  Quoted in R. Connaughton, *The War of the Rising Sun and the Tumbling Bear*, Routledge, 1988
4.  Lady Troubridge, *Memories and Reflections*
5.  S. Lee, *Edward VII a Biography Vol. 2*, MacMillan, 1925
6.  Letter, Troubridge MSS, NMM
7.  Lee, *Edward VII*
8.  ibid
9.  Troubridge naval record, NA
10. ibid
11. Letter, Troubridge MSS, NMM
12. ibid
13. Troubridge naval record, NA
14. Quoted in Ormrod, *Una Troubridge, the friend of Radclyffe Hall*
15. ibid
16. ibid
17. Troubridge obituary, *The Times*, 30 January 1926

## Chapter 7

1.  Quoted in R. Bacon, *The Life of Lord Fisher of Kilverstone*, Hodder, 1929
2.  C. Cradock, *Whispers from the Fleet*, Gieves, 1907

3. Letter, Troubridge MSS, NMM
4. ibid
5. ibid
6. Chatfield, *The Navy and Defence*
7. Quoted in Dunn, *The Scapegoat*

## Chapter 8

1. Ormrod, *Una Troubridge, the friend of Radclyffe Hall*
2. Letter, Troubridge MSS, NMM
3. ibid
4. *The Beatty Papers volume 1*, Naval Records Society, 1993
5. Quoted in Ormrod, *Una Troubridge, the friend of Radclyffe Hall*
6. Quoted in G. Miller, *The Millstone*
7. Letter to Asquith, Churchill MSS, CAC
8. Letter, Troubridge MSS, NMM, and widely quoted, e.g. R. McLaughlin, *The Escape of the* Goeben
9. Quoted in Ormrod, *Una Troubridge, the friend of Radclyffe Hall*
10. McLaughlin, *The Escape of the* Goeben
11. N.A. Lambert, *Sir John Fisher's Naval Reforms*, University of South Carolina Press, 1999

## Chapter 9

1. Quoted, *inter alia*, in McLaughlin, *The Escape of the* Goeben
2. ibid
3. Quoted in R. Hough, *The Great War at Sea*, OUP, 1983
4. ibid
5. Admiralty signal 3 August in Churchill's hand, quoted in McLaughlin, *The Escape of the* Goeben
6. Milne to Troubridge, 5 August, quoted ibid

## Chapter 11

1. Hough, *The Great War at Sea*
2. Quoted ibid
3. Quoted ibid
4. *Declaration of Capt. F. Wray, 1917*, NA
5. ibid
6. ibid
7. Quoted in Hough, *The Great War at Sea*

8. ibid
9. Troubridge MSS, NMM
10. Admiral of the Fleet Viscount Cunningham, *A Sailor's Odyssey*, Hutchinson, 1951. It is possible that he reserved his judgement on Troubridge's failure to engage because Ernest's son Tommy had served under him with distinction during Operation Torch, the invasion of French North Africa in 1943
11. ibid
12. H. Horniman, *Smiling Through*, unpublished autobiography, 1953, Horniman MSS, Imperial War Museum (IWM).
13. ibid
14. ibid
15. Phillimore MSS, IWM
16. H. Fitch, *My Misspent Youth*, Macmillan, 1937
17. Horniman MSS, IWM

## Chapter 12

1. Quoted in McLaughlin, *The Escape of the* Goeben
2. Quoted in Hough, *The Great War at Sea*
3. Quoted in G. Miller, *Superior Force*, Hull University Press, undated
4. Quoted in McLaughlin, *The Escape of the* Goeben
5. See Dunn, *The Scapegoat*

## Chapter 13

1. Quoted in McLaughlin, *The Escape of the* Goeben
2. ibid
3. Board of Admiralty Minutes, 11 December 1914, NA
4. ibid
5. ibid
6. ibid
7. ibid
8. Quoted in S. Ross, *Admiral Sir Francis Bridgeman*, Baily's, 1998
9. M. Baker, *Our Three Selves*, Hamish Hamilton, 1985
10. Adm. Sir S. Freemantle, *My Naval Career*, Hutchinson, 1949
11. *The Times*, 23 November 1914
12. Fitch, *My Misspent Youth*
13. Horniman MSS, IWM

## Chapter 14

1. Quoted in Ormrod, *Una Troubridge, the friend of Radclyffe Hall*
2. ibid
3. Letter from Una to a friend quoted in *inter alia*, Miller, *Superior Force*
4. Quoted in Dunn, *The Scapegoat*
5. *London Gazette*, 1 January 1901
6. *Declaration of Captain F. Wray, 1917*, NA
7. Letter Troubridge MSS, NMM

## Chapter 15

1. Baker, *Our Three Selves*
2. ibid
3. R. Hattersley, *The Edwardians*, Little Brown, 2004

## Chapter 16

1. Troubridge obviously held in great esteem for after the war he stood as godfather to Newman's eldest son
2. Fitch, *My Misspent Youth*
3. Haggard MSS, Vol. IV, Imperial War Museum (IWM)
4. Quoted in C. Fryer, *The Death of Serbia 1915*, Columbia University Press, 1997
5. Troubridge Serbian journal, published in Fryer, *The Death of Serbia* and now at IWM
6. ibid
7. ibid
8. ibid
9. ibid
10. ibid
11. ibid
12. ibid
13. ibid
14. ibid
15. ibid
16. ibid
17. ibid
18. ibid
19. ibid

20. R.D.G. Laffan, *Guardians at the Gate*, with a foreword by Vice-Admiral E.T. Troubridge, OUP, 1918
21. Troubridge Serbian journal

## Chapter 17

1. Ormrod, *Una Troubridge, the friend of Radclyffe Hall*
2. D. Souhami, *The Trials of Radclyffe Hall*, Weidenfeld and Nicolson, 1998
3. ibid
4. Quoted in A. Palmer, *The Gardeners of Salonika*, Faber and Faber, 1965

## Chapter 18

1. *London Gazette*, 3 June 1919
2. *London Gazette*, 14 March 1916
3. *Declaration of Captain F Wray, 1917*, NA
4. ibid
5. ibid
6. Souhami, *The Trials of Radclyffe Hall*
7. *Hansard* 1919
8. ibid
9. ibid
10. ibid
11. ibid
12. Letter to McKenna, 31 January 1921, McKenna MSS, CAC
13. ibid
14. Letter Troubridge MSS, NMM
15. Burrows MSS, Liddell-Hart archives, Kings College London (KCLA)
16. ibid
17. ibid

## Chapter 19

1. Quoted in Souhami, *The Trials of Radclyffe Hall*
2. ibid
3. *Dundee Advertiser*, 10 April 1923
4. *A Rough Account of the* Goeben *and the* Breslau, Troubridge MSS, NMM
5. ibid
6. ibid
7. ibid

## Chapter 20

1. Letter to McKenna 31 January 1921, McKenna MSS, CAC
2. ibid
3. Troubridge MSS, NMM

## Chapter 21

1. The Cunningham-Reid and Eyres-Monsell exchange in *Hansard* 1933
2. Quoted in R.K. Massie, *Castles of Steel*, Ballantine Books, 2003

## Chapter 22

1. E.T. to Milne 0225, Milne to E.T. 0323. All signals that follow are taken from the Signal Log of HMS *Defence* (IWM). All times GMT, local time one hour ahead, times given are those of the taking in or sending of the signal.
2. E.T. to Milne 1120
3. 0043
4. E.T. to squadron 0612, E.T. to Milne 1419, Milne to E.T. 1830, E.T. to Milne 1741, E.T. to ships 1654, E.T. to ships 1758
5. E.T. to *Dublin* 2112, E.T. to ships 2153,
6. E.T. to squadron 0210
7. E.T. to *Dublin/Gloucester* 0333
8. E.T. to Milne 0349, E.T. to squadron 0350, Milne to E.T. 0721
9. E.T. to Milne 1345
10. Lambert, *Admirals*
11. C. von Clausewitz, *On War*, Routledge and Kegan Paul, 1908
12. ibid
13. Quoted in Lambert, *Admirals*
14. See Chapter 13.

## Chapter 23

1. R. Dellamora, *Radclyffe Hall, a life in writing*, University of Pennsylvania Press, 2011

# Select Bibliography

The following secondary sources have been helpful in the writing of this book:

Bacon, R., *The Life of Lord Fisher of Kilverstone*, Hodder, 1929.

Baker, M., *Our Three Selves*, Hamish Hamilton, 1985.

Chatfield, Adm. A.E., *The Navy and Defence*, Heinemann, 1942.

Clausewitz, C. von, *On War*, Routledge and Kegan Paul, 1908.

Connaughton, R., *The War of the Rising Sun and the Tumbling Bear*, Routledge, 1988.

Cradock, C., *Whispers from the Fleet*, Gieves, 1907.

Cunningham, Adm. A., *A Sailor's Odyssey*, Hutchinson, 1951.

Dellamora, R., *Radclyffe Hall, a Life in Writing*, University of Pennsylvania Press, 2011.

Dunn, S.R., *The Scapegoat; the Life and Tragedy of a Fighting Admiral*, Book Guild, 2014.

Fitch, H., *My Misspent Youth*, Macmillan, 1937.

Freemantle, Adm S., *My Naval Career*, Hutchinson, 1949.

Hattersley, R., *The Edwardians*, Little Brown, 2004.

Hough, R., *The Great War at Sea*, OUP, 1983.

Laffan, R., *Guardians at the Gate*, with a foreword by Vice-Admiral E.C.T. Troubridge, OUP, 1918.

Lambert, A., *Admirals*, Faber and Faber, 2008.

Lambert, N.A., *Sir John Fishers Naval Reforms*, University of South Carolina Press, 1999.

Lee, S., *Edward VII, a Biography Volume 2*, Macmillan, 1925.

MacLaughlin, R., *The Escape of the* Goeben, Seeley Service, 1974.

McGibbon, I., *Blue Water Rationale*, G.P. Print, NZ.

Miller, G., *The Millstone*, web published.

Miller, G., *Superior Force*, Hull University Press (undated).

Ormrod, R., *Una Troubridge, the Friend of Radclyffe Hall*, Jonathan Cape, 1984.

Parker, A., *The Gardeners of Salonika*, Faber and Faber, 1965.

# SELECT BIBLIOGRAPHY

Penrose-Fitzgerald, C., *From Steam to Sail*, E. Arnold, 1922.
Rose, K., *King George V*, Weidenfeld and Nicolson, 1983.
Ross, S., *Admiral Sir Francis Bridgeman*, Bailys, 1998.
Souhami, D., *The Trials of Radclyffe Hall*, Weidenfeld and Nicolson, 1998.
Troubridge, Lady L., *Memories and Reflections*, Heinemann, 1928.
Waterhouse, M., *Edwardian Requiem*, Biteback Publishing, 2013.

# Index

Page references in *italic* indicate illustrations.